TRILLION DOLLAR TRAINWRECK

How The F-35 Hollowed Out The U.S. Air Force

Bill Sweetman

Arlington, Virginia

www.valkstrat.com

TRILLION DOLLAR TRAINWRECK

How The F-35 Hollowed Out The U.S. Air Force

ISBN: 9798324580780
Imprint: Independently published

CONTENTS

Bill Sweetman brings a unique perspective to the long-running Joint Strike Fighter project. He was the only reporter present at the signature of the original U.K.-U.S. ASTOVL MoU ten years before that, and was among the project's closest observers for the next three decades, breaking many stories and earning multiple awards. He wrote two books on JSF[1] and was a consultant to an Emmy-winning documentary on the project[2] before spending seven years as a strategist with a major JSF partner company. He provides consulting services through Valkyrie Strategic Solutions LLC.

---

[1] Joint Strike Fighter, Motorbooks 1999; Ultimate Fighter, Zenith 2004

[2] Battle of the X-Planes, Nova, 2001

PREFACE

"If you don't follow the defense business closely, then you can be excused for believing that the F-35 Joint Strike Fighter is in trouble"[3], wrote a well-connected backer of the multi-service project late in 2009. Two months later, the program director was fired, and an entirely new leadership team was appointed to stabilize the program and arrive at a new and attainable schedule, a process that took three more years.

The F-35 effort has been characterized from its early years by such conflicting views and conflicting realities. This report is both an update on the controversy and an attempt to explain why this is so.

Hundreds of F-35s are in service. The fighter is being produced at a rate higher than has been seen since the early 1990s, at a procurement cost (for the F-35A model) comparable to other aircraft that do not feature the F-35's stealth technology. Its pilots report that they consider the aircraft lethal and effective. It remains unbeaten on the export market.

The F-35 has nonetheless been a strategic failure.

Strategy is above all the matching of goals to resources, so few people would or should disagree with this: the purpose of defense acquisition should not be to design and build airplanes (or ships or tanks), or to sustain defense contractors, but to design and equip a force that deters the adversary, to support and arm allies, and to do so in a way that aligns both with military objectives and with diplomatic and economic realities.

The F-35 has failed because the program was not designed to do that. In its formative years, there was no visible near-term threat that would justify a large military force. The program's purpose was to

[3] https://www.lexingtoninstitute.org/four-reasons-for-confidence-in-the-f-35/

maintain the ability to rebuild that force if it became necessary, by insuring the survival of an industrial and technological base.

The result was the development of an "all things to all people" project, that was not well matched to the needs that did emerge – but at the same time cut off the oxygen for any alternative approach, so that it remained the central pillar of air combat acquisition. As Eberhardt Rechtin famously put it: "All the serious mistakes are made in the first day"[4].

Nobody today can argue that the U.S. and allied TacAir force is as effective, compared to the adversary, as it was when the program started in 1996. It is routinely stated that the U.S. Air Force's TacAir fleet is dangerously weak, and that the fighter force is "geriatric"[5]. Todd Harrison, Washington's acknowledged budget guru, says the force is in "a death spiral."[6]

In June 2023, the Air Force Association's Mitchell Institute issued a report[7] that sounded the alarm.

"The Air Force is the oldest, smallest, and least ready in its entire history… [it] now possesses a fighter inventory that is geriatric and on the brink of inadequacy."

The Mitchell report had one overriding recommendation: go all-in on F-35 Block 4, the latest development of the aircraft, and accelerate production concurrently with development. Mitchell is well-

[4] The Art of Systems Architecting; Eberhardt Rechtin, Mark W. Maier

[5] "We have a geriatric Air Force," Lt Gen Dave Deptula (USAF, Ret.), 2012. Dan Parsons, "The Air Force Trades Quantity for Quality," National Defense Magazine, March 1, 2012.

[6] "As the US Air Force fleet keeps shrinking, can it still win wars?", Defense News, April 24, 2024

[7] "Accelerating 5th Generation Airpower: Bringing Capability and Capacity to the Merge" by Lt Gen Joseph Guastella, Douglas Birkey, and Lt Col Eric Gunzinger

connected and there is little doubt that the conclusion is shared by industry and by air force seniors.

The report made two errors. The first was to assume that the F-35 program could deliver in its promises now when it had failed to do so in the past. The second was to obscure the fact that the F-35 program's performance was the cause of the service's problems, claiming that "the Air Force has not received the funding necessary to procure a sufficient volume of new fighters that would ensure the outflow of aging aircraft." As for slower-than-expected F-35 deliveries, the report attributed this to "mainly budget-driven decisions."

The USAF alone expected to buy 110 F-35s per year at the project's inception , completing production in FY2026. That target has receded by 25 years.

This is entirely incorrect, as little as the authors - from an industry-sponsored think tank – may wish to say so. The USAF has spent $192 billion on the F-35 and its F-22 stablemate since 1997 but the number of aircraft delivered so far is a fraction of what was intended. The final F-35 delivery for the USAF will be at least 25 years later than planned[8], the aircraft delivered are not satisfactory, and R&D costs for fixes and improvements are running at levels comparable to all-new programs.

Meanwhile, the rest of the force continues to age out, with F-16s expected to reach more than 40 years of service before they are replaced. At the time of writing, almost 100 new F-35s are in storage at an undisclosed location, because delays to testing mean that they cannot be delivered[9]; and when they are delivered, it will be another

[8] GAO 23-106047, May 2023. Primary sources for earlier planned delivery schedules are Selected Acquisition Reports, found at https://www.esd.whs.mil/FOIA/Reading-Room/Reading-Room-List_2/Selected_Acquisition_Reports/

12-16 months before they receive vital combat capabilities. Moreover, a major multi-year upgrade project has been effectively canceled, its schedule deemed unattainable, and a less comprehensive program is being defined[10].

There are many causes for the delays, but the overarching problem has been pressure from the contractors to maintain the pace of the program despite serious technical problems, combined with a lack of control by the Joint Program Office (JPO) and short-sighted unwillingness of the end users to acknowledge the issues.

One result is that more than 1,000 aircraft already delivered will require major modifications costing tens of millions of dollars per aircraft if they are to remain in service, and it is likely that many older aircraft will be beyond the point where they can be economically upgraded, and will be retired early.

The U.S. program was also expected to secure the nation's dominance of the combat aircraft business and to make the allied force more closely interoperable. This has been partly accomplished in the short term. But some allies will have mixed fleets of F-35s and other aircraft that are not easily interoperable at all. The three "EuroCanard" projects[11] that the F-35 was expected to replace are alive and kicking, Korea and Turkey have credible indigenous fighter programs, and Japan – almost entirely reliant on U.S.-designed aircraft since post-WW2 rearmament started in 1956 – has joined the British-led Global Combat Aircraft Program, one of two European projects for post-F-35 fighters.

Evaluating the combat effectiveness of the F-35, relative either to competitors or adversary defense systems, is not the main focus of

---

[9] https://www.forbes.com/sites/erictegler/2024/01/25/the-dealer-lot-is-fullwhere-is-lockheed-martin-storing-f-35s/?sh=7cb9d0032f4e

[10] https://armedservices.house.gov/hearings/tal-hearing-fiscal-year-2025-budget-request-department-defense-fixed-wing-tactical-and

[11] Dassault Rafale, Eurofighter Typhoon and Saab Gripen

this report but is addressed in an appendix, acknowledging the fact that it is an open-source intelligence exercise involving assumptions and guesses about classified technologies.

But it is telling that the USAF was offered the option to install an all-new engine in future and retrofitted F-35s, greatly improving performance (including a dramatic 30% range increase), and has turned it down, in favor of upgrading the current engine, which provides very little improvement at all. If the lofty claims of all-domain supremacy made for the F-35 were valid, re-engining the F-35 should offer a higher return on investment in the 2028-35 timeframe; but the USAF is selecting the latter course.

There have also been suggestions that the U.S. should acquire a new combat aircraft, smaller and less costly than the F-35, to bolster force numbers and pilot development[12]. The USAF has been directed to produce a new force design[13] including fighters and unmanned aircraft through 2036.

That is why this report is timely. Major decisions are now being taken, in the U.S. and elsewhere, on programs that are intended to redress the balance of conventional deterrence through air power, sometime in the 2030s. These include the Next Generation Air Dominance (NGAD) program for the U.S. Air Force and the F/A-XX for the Navy, both of which face uncertain futures in mid-2024. Outside the U.S., the UK-Italy-Japan Global Combat Air Program (GCAP) is going ahead, alongside multiple unmanned combat air vehicle projects.

The U.S. and its allies that depend on it can neither afford to repeat this experience nor abandon innovation. So far there has been no

---

[12] Few people on the program today were there when it was known as the Common Affordable Lightweight Fighter.

[13] https://www.airandspaceforces.com/congress-air-force-space-force-force-design-2050/

public attempt to analyze the factors that have led to the program's delays, cost increases, and deficiencies in performance.

The F-35 program has enjoyed abundant resources to tell its story. The communications staffs of its prime contractors outnumber the editorial staff of any trade media group. Service-members are schooled in program talking points[14]. Critics have been few, often contemptuously if amusingly labelled as Cassandras[15]. This study offers a counterpoint to the orthodox view. It is based on documentation, data and realistic analysis.

Team F-35 sometimes bristles at mentions of a trillion-dollar program. But the first use of that number was by Lockheed Martin aeronautics president Micky Blackwell, in January 1996. "The JAST program could end up being a trillion-dollar program. We are talking lots of planes, a lot of money."[16] He was right, at least about the money.

---

[14] Downloaded from militarytimes.com

[15] The curse that Apollo laid upon Cassandra, as people often forget, is that she would prophesy the truth and never be believed.

[16] Theresa Hitchens and Frank Oliveri, "Company Predicts Windfall for JAST Winner," Defense News (January 29, 1996),

STRATEGIC FAILURE

The principal strategic shortfall of the F-35 program is that its development has been delayed by unpredicted and ill-managed technical issues, and its unit procurement and operating costs have exceeded early and optimistic estimates. This has slowed the ramp-up of production and forced the customer to reduce production rates, both to stay within budget and to avoid building flawed and immature aircraft that require costly retrofits in order to meet requirements.[17]

When the F-35 program took shape in 1995, the F-35 and the F-22 were intended to constitute the entire fighter force by the late 2020s, with 442 Raptors and 1,763 F-35s. The USAF alone expected to buy 110 F-35s per year, completing production in FY2026. That target has receded by 25 years. The planned rate was cut to 80/year in the early 2000s (Fig.1), to 60 in 2018 and 48 in 2019[18].

Fig. 1 TacAir Recapitalization Plan 4/2010

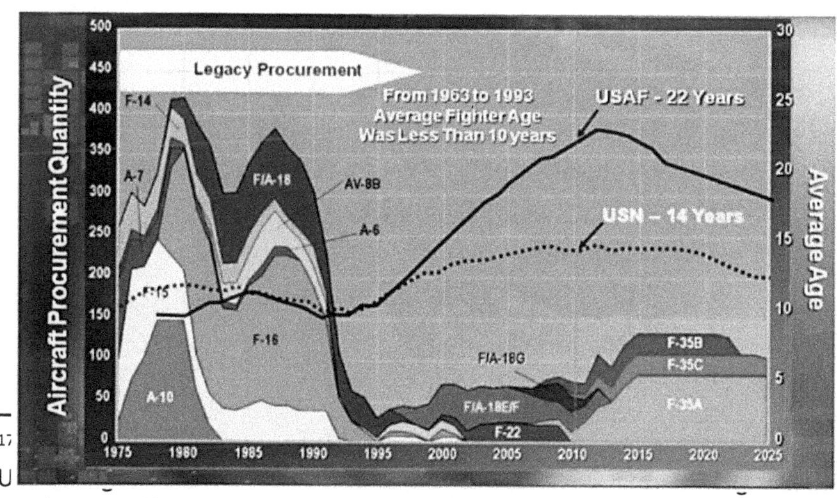

17 …

U… numbers, and by the time the operationally acceptable F-111E and F-111F versions were developed, budgets were exhausted.

18 Selected Acquisition Reports and budget documents

19 Early Block 20 F-22s could not affordably be upgraded to combat-ready Block 30s.

Further restricting replacements, the F-22 program was cut back and yielded 146 operational aircraft[19], forcing the USAF to retain its oldest F-15s long past their planned retirement dates.

Table 1: USAF has spent $192bn on fighters since 1997

Budget Line	$m
F-22 acquisition	75387
F-35 acquisition	116872
Total	192259
586 F-35 + 146 F-22 = 732	
PAUC for 732 aircraft	**279**

Source: P-1 and R-1 books, Selected Acquisition Reports

Through 2024, acquisition of the F-22 and F-35 has cost the USAF $192 billion[20] or $279 million per operational aircraft (Table 1). Until the acquisition of a few new F-15s, this monopolized the budget for new fighter aircraft, and forced the USAF to scrimp on investments, such as modernizing its F-16 and F-15 fleets, not to mention deferring the replacement of vital support assets such as the E-3 AWACS fleet[21], which was allowed to decay and now is obsolescent.

Since 2001, the existing USAF TacAir fleet has been extensively used and deployed in support of combat operations, and is literally wearing out. "The bulk of the service's fighter fleet consists of A-10Cs, F-15C/Ds, and F-16C/Ds designed in the 1960s and 1970s," the Air Force Association's Mitchell Institute reported in 2023. "They were mainly produced in the 1970s and 1980s, and now they are averaging 41, 38, and 32 years of age, respectively. Newer types, such as the F-15E, average 30 years old."[22]

---

[20] In then-year dollars, based on budget documents and Selected Acquisition Reports. Thes numbers do not include the 50% share of R&D paid by the Navy. F-22 and F-35 PAUC document

[21] At one point AWACS replacement was put off until 2035, until it was realized that the system was no longer fit for purpose in WestPac and a hurried program to acquire the E-7 Wedgetail was put in place.

[22] https://mitchellaerospacepower.org/wp-

In 2023, Air Force leaders testified, "the 179 F-15C/Ds in the Air Force's inventory will reach the end of their design service life in the next five to seven years, and our analysis shows additional service life extension programs are not cost-effective."[23] The lack of fighter capacity due to aging aircraft and other reasons is why the Air Force was forced to withdraw F-15C/Ds from the strategically vital Kadena Air Base in Okinawa in late 2022.

F-35 costs are not easy to extract from the thousands of pages of budget documentation that the Pentagon produces each year. F-35 costs for the Air Force are listed in multiple line items for development, production, and modification of existing aircraft (Table 2). Some early aircraft will not be fully operational, so that has to be taken into account. But in all, the USAF will have spent $199m in

Table 2: Each F-35 through 2027 delivery costs the USAF $199m

Budget Line (USAF costs only)	$m (TY)	Source
EMD	29854	FY24 budget
C2D2 thru 2021	1497	FY21 budget
C2D2 2022-24	3394	FY24 budget
C2D2 FY25	1124	FY25 Budget
F-35 Squadrons to 2021	1437	FY21 budget
F-35 Squadrons 2022-25	268	FY25 budget
Procurement	76299	FY25 budget
F-35 Modifications	2999	FY25 budget
Total acquisition	116872	
633 funded thru 2025 - 47 Lot 1-6 = 586		
PAUC for 544 aircraft through 2025	**199**	

program acquisition unit cost (PAUC) for every operational F-35 delivered through 2027.[24]

---

content/uploads/2023/06/Accelerating_Fifth_Generation_Airpower_Policy_Paper_43-FINAL.pdf

[23] Senate Armed Services Committee (SASC), Hon. Andrew P. Hunter, Assistant Secretary of the Air Force (Acquisition, Technology & Logistics), "Presentation to the SASC Subcommittee on Airland on Air Force, Force Structure and Modernization Programs," March 29, 2023, p. 13.

[24] Deliveries generally take place two years after the funding year.

The cost picture for the Department of the Navy (DoN) F-35 program is further complicated because the Navy lists the short take-off, vertical landing (STOVL) F-35B variant and the carrier-based (CV) F-35C separately. PAUC has been higher, at $344 million (Table 3), but strategic effects have been different.

Table 3: Each Navy F-35B/C through 2027 is a $344M investment

Budget Line	$m (TY)	Source
EMD (USN)	51171	FY24 budget
F-35B C2D2 2022-25	2059	FY25 budget
F-35C C2D2 2022-25	1987	FY25 budget
F-35C Procurement Inc USMC to 2024	36421	FY25 budget +13
F-35B Procurement to 2024	29365	FY25 budget
Total acquisition	121003	
408 funded thru 2024 - 56 Lot 1-6 = 352		
PAUC for 326 aircraft through 2024	**344**	

The Marine Corps STOVL force is in any case less important to most campaigns than the Navy's, and its relative value has declined over the years because the Corps, fixated on F-35, declined to acquire F/A-18E/F Super Hornets and eked more hours out of obsolete F/A-18C Hornets and AV-8Bs.

The U.S. Navy fighter force has aged less because the Navy continued to buy Boeing F/A-18E/F Super Hornets and EA-18G Growlers, in successively improved variants, while the service waited for the F-35C to be available. However, the weight and drag of the Navy variant escalated well beyond expectations, compromising performance[25]. Until early 2024, the Navy appeared headed for an early switch of production from the F-35C to the follow-on F/A-XX, which would initially replace Super Hornets, but that program has been delayed.

---

[25] Transonic acceleration time in particular has been affected. Since transonic acceleration requires full afterburner, long acceleration times reduce the time that the airplane can spend at supersonic speed. Some sources have suggested that for practical purposes, the F-35C is barely supersonic.

From 1996 through the current defense budget (FY2025) the USAF and U.S. Navy have spent $238 billion on development and production of the F-35, for a 938 operational aircraft[26] - $254 million each (Table 4).

Table 4: Each US F-35 delivered through 2027 has cost $254m

Budget Line	$m (TY)	Source
DoN acquisition	121003	
USAF acquisition	116872	
Total acquisition	237875	
DoN 352 + USAF 586	938	
PAUC for 938 aircraft through 2025	**254**	

PAUC presents one view of program cost: the total investment up to the current point in time to put hardware on the flightline. Normally, PAUC peaks at the start of production and then declines steeply as R&D spending slows and stops and more production aircraft are built. But this will not happen quickly with the F-35, for two reasons[27].

The first is that the F-35 program is still in concurrent R&D and production, 22 years after the engineering and manufacturing development contract was released. The Block 4 version, which is the first that the Air Force considers to be adequate for operations against the late-2020s threat, had an estimated R&D budget of $16.5 billion[28] in late 2023 (53% of the all-new B-21 bomber's R&D cost[29]). More recently, Block 4 has run into massive problems. In December 2023, Lt. Gen. Michael Schmidt, the program executive officer for the F-35, said that he could not predict when a software issue that

[26] This number excludes pre-TR-2 aircraft, which are not expected to be upgraded.

[27] As this revised edition is being written, the PAUC is increasing because money is being spent, but no aircraft delivered.

[28] This is the figure listed in the tables as C2D2 (Continuous Capability and Development Delivery (C2D2)

[29] Budget documents and CRS reports

had halted aircraft deliveries since July would be corrected. "I wish I had all of the solutions in place that prove to me that when I do something in the lab, it's going to show up that way in the air," Schmidt told a Congressional panel.[30]

In April 2024 Schmidt disclosed that the Block 4 plan had effectively failed. Deliveries would not resume until August/September, but with a "truncated" version of the first Block 4 version (which was originally scheduled to be delivered, in full, in the final quarter of 2023) – which will not be combat-capable. "Certain capabilities are not available" in the truncated version, Schmidt told a Congressional panel, and they will not arrive for another 12-16 months – the final quarter of 2025 at best. That is a two-year slip in one calendar year, and it means that no combat-capable aircraft will have been delivered for more than two years.

Schmidt also told the panel that the entire multi-year Block 4 program was being "reimagined" because it had been re-examined and found to be not feasible, and would deliver only the most critically needed capabilities rather than the planned 80-plus. In an updated briefing on May 16, it was disclosed that.:

"The program office anticipates the scope of Block 4 will change as it becomes a major subprogram by removing capabilities that cannot be supported by the current F-35 engine and thermal management system... Program officials stated that the earliest the program expects to deliver post-Block 4 capabilities is 2029."[31]

Moreover, the F-35 requires a revised engine and new power and thermal management system to support the thermal loads of the Block 4 avionics. No complete R&D budget has been published for this effort. Adding up three line items in the C2D2 budgets gives $1.4 billion in propulsion development through FY2029, the last year listed.

---

[30] https://aviationweek.com/defense-space/aircraft-propulsion/f-35-delivery-freeze-complicated-software-doubts-hardware

[31] House Armed Services Committee testimony

The second reason that the F-35 will remain expensive is that all these new features have to be retrofitted to many of the nearly-1,000 F-35s that have already been delivered.

As well as re-equipping U.S. and allied air forces, the F-35 was to support other strategic goals.

Reduce sustainment costs: The JSF program was expected to reduce lifetime sustainment costs of the fighter force through new technology. But costs remain higher than earlier types, with a September 2023 Government Accountability Office report showing conflict between the contractors' rights to IP and the need to transition maintenance to government depots[32] was driving workload upward, and that the Joint Program Office had no plan to address this problem.

Make the defense industry more efficient: A further overt aim was to force the development of a more efficient and more competitive U.S. defense industry: with fewer high-value programs, contractors would have to merge, diversify or downsize. There was indeed a massive wave of mergers and acquisitions, but rather than increasing the intensity of competition or fostering innovation, it created a small group of powerful, integrated prime contractors. Faced with more recent DoD cost-cutting initiatives, these companies have found that protecting their existing programs has higher margins and lower risk than competing for new business, let alone investing in innovative concepts.

Consolidate global industrial superiority: JSF was launched with the expectation that it would replace U.S. and European fighters in allied and aligned air forces. But in the past decade, foreign nations that had the ability to prime a fighter aircraft have launched new fighter programs, along with life-extension measures for existing products, along with future programs. Japan, which was long

---

[32] F-35 Aircraft: DOD and the Military Services Need to Reassess the Future Sustainment Strategy; GAO-23-105341

exclusively partnered with the U.S. for fighters and other defense technology, has signed a co-development agreement with the UK and Italy, and the Republic of Korea and Turkey are developing their first indigenous fighters.

Even at this point, the path to a highly common global fleet is uncertain as to both schedule and cost. Almost 1,000 aircraft have been delivered in a working but immature configuration (Tech Refresh 2/Block 3) and will have to be upgraded or replaced.

Deliver common, versatile aircraft for three services. The three F-35 variants are by now different airplanes sharing common avionics and (for the F-35A and F-35C) common propulsion. The F-35B STOVL variant, which imposed the most onerous restrictions on the F-35's design of all three versions, was intended to be used from LHA/LHD amphibious warfare ships and from improvised, short-runway bases ashore, like the preceding AV-8B Harrier. However, it cannot perform vertical landings ashore except on specially built concrete pads, because of the heat and velocity of the aft exhaust.

The true strategic cost of STOVL is that it contributed far more to increased cost and delays, and led to degraded capability of all versions, than is generally appreciated – in return for 60 uniquely deployable aircraft[33].

[33] The Navy has a goal of 11 America-class LHA ships of which at most 10 will be deployable at any time, with a normal aircraft complement including six F-35Bs.

DAY-ONE MISTAKES

The F-35 program's strategic goals were established in 1994-95, before any contracts were issued. They were ambitious, and the difficulties facing the program were underestimated. The objective of replacing almost the entire U.S. fighter inventory is well known and sometimes discussed as if it was the only objective, but there were other important aims.

The primary objective was to **replace the entire U.S. tactical air inventory**, except for the Lockheed Martin F-22 and the F/A-18E/F Super Hornet, which were still under development. This was ambitious, given that the sole previous attempt to develop a common USAF/Navy fighter, the F-111, had failed[34], and the JSF was to replace a much wider range of aircraft, with three rather than two variants. But planners expected that higher production rates and a larger force would spread non-recurring costs over larger numbers of aircraft, permit more efficient production, and lead to a common support system and supply chain. The key was to develop a specification that met the high end of the USAF and Navy requirements while being practical for a STOVL aircraft.

The JSF **would field very low observable (VLO) technology**[35] across most of the tactical aviation force by 2020. No other nation had even tested a VLO aircraft in 1995. VLO-across-the-force was a new idea even in the U.S.; through the 1980s, plans envisaged a mix of VLO and non-VLO aircraft, and the move to all-VLO was controversial within the USAF.[36] JSF promised to deliver VLO at little if any extra cost, through economies of scale.

---

[34] The Navy's version of the F-111 was canceled before any production aircraft had been delivered. The McDonnell Douglas F-4 and Vought A-7 had been used by the USAF and Navy, but both were fully developed for the Navy before being ordered for the Air Force.

[35] VLO implies reducing signatures over multiple frequency bands all around the aircraft, and demands all-internal weapon and fuel carriage

[36] Gen Mike Loh, leader of Air Combat Command, recommended in 1993 that

The JSF was the mechanism to bring about a sharp **reduction in the number of military aircraft prime contractors.** The company or team winning JSF would win most of U.S. TacAir spending through the 2010s, enforcing the plan that had been outlined by Deputy Defense Secretary William Perry at the July 1993 "Last Supper" meeting with defense contractors[37]. Perry and other defense leaders realized that the end of the Cold War meant that the U.S. no longer had a major adversary and that the defense industry needed to be reshaped to survive a loss of business on the same scale as in 1919 and 1946.

JSF was intended to **improve the U.S. position in the global combat aircraft market** from leadership to near-total dominance. F-16s, F/A-18s and F-15s had been widely exported, including to markets where European suppliers had a foothold. Importantly, this was the first time that most export customers had flown the same aircraft as U.S. forces. DoD planners expected that by offering VLO and partnership in a 3,000-plus-unit program, the U.S. could pre-empt sales of the new fighters under development in Europe[38]. The STOVL version played a strategic role, because Britain and Italy wanted to maintain their maritime air power, but developing a STOVL aircraft to replace the Anglo-U.S. Harrier was not economical unless the U.S. Marine Corps was a customer; and Britain and Italy were partners in the Eurofighter project, which was in political and technical trouble in 1995.[39] Bringing them into JSF

---

the next step in fighter development should involve much improved versions of the F-16 and F-15, incorporating some LO technology. Chief of Staff Gen Merrill (Tony) McPeak favored an all-VLO force, and his view prevailed.

[37] https://www.washingtonpost.com/archive/business/1997/07/04/how-a-dinner-led-to-a-feeding-frenzy/13961ba2-5908-4992-8335-c3c087cdebc6/

[38] By the mid-90s, the Dassault Rafale, Eurofighter Typhoon and Saab Gripen were all flying.

[39] With the end of the Cold War and the costs of German re-unification, politics in that country – the co-leading partner in Eurofighter with the UK – swung against heavy defense investments, and there was a long delay in approval for the Eurofighter production contract. The prototype aircraft were also

would be a direct threat to Eurofighter, given that the other major partner, Germany, was wavering in its commitment.

Another JSF goal **was to stop, or even reverse, the geometric growth in military aircraft unit cost** that aerospace executive Norm Augustine had observed and codified as his sixteenth Law[40], along with the rise in operating cost that was increasingly stressing air forces. JSF was intended to take advantage of a computer-driven revolution in the way that military aircraft were designed, built, and sustained, using techniques such as lean manufacturing, design-anywhere-build-anywhere, high-speed machining, and advanced composites. Aircraft usage would be tracked by a computer system to predict failures, and just-in-time spares supply would replace large spares stockpiles sitting mostly idle at operational bases.

Most of these strategic goals had built-in problems.

Working as a strategist, the author developed a principle: Every strategy needs a Plan B, and that Plan B must be better than "so then we retreat to Smolensk, where we all starve to death in a snowbank". The JSF, as the sole future U.S. fighter program, not only had no formal Plan B, but as it proceeded, alternative plans would be harder to contemplate because the nation's ability to develop new combat aircraft would start to atrophy.

An early casualty of the JSF project was a promising international venture to develop a much-improved version of the F-16 with a delta wing; the USAF would not provide the support that it needed.[41] And if the project was terminated or truncated, the Pentagon would have

---

experiencing problems with handling characteristics.

[40] Law Number XVI states that: 'In the year 2054, the entire defense budget will purchase just one aircraft. This aircraft will have to be shared by the Air Force and Navy 3–1/2 days each per week except for the leap year, when it will be made available to the Marines for the extra day"

[41] The so-called F-16U was a delta-winged aircraft for the United Arab Emirates, its development funded by the UAE. However, the Mideast nation required the USAF to buy one wing (72 aircraft) of the type, but having already rejected the Loh proposal (footnote 2) the USAF would not do this.

to fund multiple replacements for the three U.S. services and export partners. As JSF progressed through development and into production, too, the industry's ability to design and build another combat aircraft, whether a competitor or a follow-on type, would atrophy. The project became, almost literally, "too big to fail" – a term originally applied to major financial institutions in crisis, that truly means "too big to be allowed to fail, regardless of cost to the taxpayer."

Program leaders committed very early to building a single design – a common outer mold line – as the basis for JSF. Other ways to achieve economies of scale, such as using common components and systems in mission-tailored variants[42], were not assessed at all. Economies of scale were also offset by higher non-recurring engineering costs and performance penalties.

By the 1990s, the cost of engineering VLO into an aircraft design, and making it producible, was indeed lower than it had been in the 1980s. What was not appreciated in the formative months of the JSF program was the degree to which VLO would drive cost not only into design and production, but also into operations and sustainment.

The JSF program did play an important role in precipitating the Last Supper process of consolidation, but the DoD had little control over how that unfolded. In the three-way competition for two JSF demonstration-phase contracts, Boeing emerged as a surprise winner, precipitating Boeing's acquisition of McDonnell Douglas[43].

The security issues surrounding VLO were even more important for export markets, the technology being one of the Pentagon's crown jewels. But the security issues related to exporting JSFs to foreign nations were at best skated over, possibly because there was no peer

---

[42] The author in the late 1990s pointed out that this was how Airbus was growing its product line.

[43] This may have been one of the largest single unpredictable impacts of the program, since McDonnell Douglas management took control of Boeing Commercial Airplanes and transformed it radically.

technological adversary at the time and no sign that one would emerge.

Augustine had not attempted to identify the reasons for the rising cost of combat aircraft, beyond observing that it appeared to be independent of production rate. It is the author's contention that the rising cost is related to both size (operating empty weight being the best surrogate measure) and complexity.

Complexity is not just when a vehicle (or any other system) has many subsystems or functions. Complexity increases as subsystems and functions interact with other subsystems, which they may do in multiple domains, including thermal, electromagnetic, mechanical, energetic, and informational. The level of complexity is related to the number of interactions rather than the number of subsystems.

For example, the post-WW2 B-36 bomber (produced in the same factory as the F-35 today) was complicated. Its six main engines had 28 cylinders and were turbosupercharged, and it had four jet booster engines. It could defend itself with sixteen 20-mm. autocannon in eight turrets, remotely aimed by a fire control computer. It featured radar and electronic warfare systems. But all these things functioned independently, aside from electrical power, and were "integrated" by the 15-man crew.

The baseline level of equipment for the successful U.S. teen-series fighters was set by the McDonnell Douglas F-4, the most successful U.S. supersonic fighter of the 1950s and 1960s. The USAF's F-4E was one of the first aircraft to be identified as a "strike fighter" capable of air-to-air and air-to-ground missions, and featured a multi-mode radar, an inertial navigation system and an array of guided weapons. It was large and complicated by the standards of the day, but with limited *complexity*, the subsystems were independent, each had its own display, and "integration" happened in the heads of the pilot and weapon system operator.

Introduced two decades after the F-4E, the F-15E Strike Eagle typified increasing complication, with added sensors (passive RF, and infra-red in pods) and countermeasures. But each sensor had its own electronic display screen, and the system was once again integrated by the crew, who directly controlled flightpath and weapon release.

By the time JSF was being defined, the F-22 had been under development for ten years. Although its supersonic cruise and stealth technology attracted most attention, it represented a radical change in the way that information sources - radar, passive RF, and offboard sensing via datalink - were combined[44]. For example, signals from the electronic surveillance measures system could, via the central computer, change the airplane's track to present its "best side" to a hostile radar. It represented a vast but under-recognized increase in complexity, and this resulted in a very long development process.

JSF planners placed their faith, publicly, in a cost-reducing doctrine known as "cost as an independent variable" (CAIV). This called for "should-cost" targets (procurement and sustainment) to be set at the start of a major acquisition program and flowed down through system, subsystem and component design. The targets could be met by relaxing requirements, by finding ways to work more efficiently, by introducing new technology or by any other means. In the words of a contemporary essay[45]: "In some ways CAIV suffers from the combination of too many initiatives to be easily explained."

But it was too late to use the most powerful CAIV tool - the ability to balance system requirements against cost. By the time the Concept Demonstration phase was under contract, attributes such as vehicle performance, signatures, and weapon integration had been defined as KPPs for the production airplane. The demonstrator aircraft were

[44] The sensor-fusion and EMCON functions of the F-22 avionics system were summarized by the author in "F-22 Raptor", ch3, Motorbooks International 1998

[45] "Cost as an independent variable: concepts and risks". Dr Benjamin Rush, Acquisition Review Quarterly, Spring 1997

designed according to the KPPs, and to the extent that the Preferred Weapon System Concept (PWSC) vehicle design diverged from the X-plane, the point of the demonstration program would be lost, and risk increased. The only publicly discussed change to the KPPs during the CDA phase made the requirement more demanding - an increase to the Navy's bring-back load, which forced Boeing to abandon its delta wing configuration.

A Google nGram search shows that CAIV faded rapidly out of use after 2001.

HOPES, DREAMS, AND PET ROCKS

The F-35 program was launched in 1996, and approved for full-scale development in 2001, with a set of key performance parameters (KPPs) and other requirements that were considered to be balanced and realistic. The challenges had been underestimated. The combination of stealth and STOVL was much harder than expected, as was the development of an avionics system for a stealthy multi-role fighter. On the other side of the ledger, too much faith was placed in unproven technologies as a way to reduce cost.

Something that was not fully appreciated in the definition of the KPPs was what has been called "requirements compounding"[46]. This heuristic postulates that the overall impact on performance, weight, or cost, of two or more requirements combined together, will be greater than the sum of their individual impacts. For example, a dual-cycle STOVL aircraft like the F-35B has extra inlets and exhaust nozzles, which add weight. But if it is stealthy, those features must be concealed in wingborne flight by large actuated doors that must fit precisely and securely. Neither a stealthy aircraft nor a STOVL type needs those doors – only an aircraft with both attributes. Another example is the requirement for both internal weapons – resulting in a larger body volume – and supersonic speed.

Some requirements could be defined as "superdrivers", affecting many aspects of the design at a fundamental level. Stealth, at the level specified for JSF, mandates internal weapon and fuel carriage. This was well understood at the start of the program and was reflected in limited requirements for internal weapons: two precision-guided bombs and two AMRAAMs, approximating to an F-117 with added self-defense capability. Nevertheless, stealth pushed empty weight upwards – the F-35A weighs as much, empty, as the F-4E, and the latter carried the weight penalty of carrier basing.

[46] Technology For Quality and Quantity In A New Fighter, W.E. Maillard, Northrop, 1981

One stealth-related issue that was not fully appreciated was thermal management. With much more installed thrust than the subsonic F-117, and a full suite of avionics rather than passive IR alone, the JSF would have to shed much more heat.

The stealth-related issue that had the greatest impact on development cost and risk was the avionics system. It had been recognized in the F-22 program that a stealth aircraft could not have an air-to-air capability without minimizing its use of active radar; if it used its radar as a conventional fighter did, it would betray its location no matter how low its radar cross-section might be. Emissions control (EMCON) meant passive and active sensor fusion, while integrating sensor, navigation, communications and countermeasures functions in real time. Such a system required processing power that, at the time, could only be provided by a centralized airborne supercomputer, with sensors and communications subsystems as peripherals.

The same architecture was specified for JSF, with the added complexity of two electro-optical systems. It was still anticipated that the system would be easier to upgrade than a traditional "federated" architecture, partly because of a prevailing "it's only software" attitude. Planners expected the system to have an open architecture, to be based on commercial technology, and to be upgradable on the flight line by changing cards in the dual integrated common processor racks[47]. F-22 development would prove them wrong - but not until the 2000s, by which time the F-35 was committed to a similar architecture.

STOVL and the associated requirement to operate from two existing ship classes[48] determined more key features of the design than is

---

[47] International Defense Review, June 1995

[48] The U.S. Navy's LHA/LHD class and the Royal Navy's Invincible-class. There was not even a commitment to a future RN carrier when the CDA phase started, and it was expected that the F-35B would first replace the Harrier on the *Invincible*-class carriers (with a UK IOC in 2011-12) before those ships were

often appreciated – even though one of those classes would be scrapped long before the type entered service.

The Marine Corps requirement was to park six F-35s aft of the island on LHA/LHD ships. This constrained the wingspan to 35 feet. The Royal Navy's *Invincibles'* 55-foot-long mid-deck elevator restricted the overall length to around 52 feet[49]. Given the airplane's weight, power, and internal payload, this resulted in a lower fineness ratio (length to cross-sectional area) than is usual for supersonic fighters. For example, the F-35 is shorter (discounting its protruding tails) than the JAS 39 Gripen, which is barely more than half its weight. Low fineness ratio is associated with high drag, particularly in the transonic region.

STOVL mandated a single engine. It is next to impossible to design a twin-engine vertical-landing aircraft that can survive an engine failure during powered-lift flight, because the center of lift moves so far off the center of gravity that the airplane is uncontrollable. Hence, twin engines make a STOVL aircraft less rather than more safe, by doubling the chance of a catastrophic failure. The engine also had to be very large (52 inches in diameter) and installed unusually far forward so that the aircraft would be balanced in jet-lift flight. Consequently, the major systems and components housed in the mid-body section are wrapped in a complex arrangement around the engine tunnel, which is also a hot and noisy environment.

While weight is important for any aircraft, a STOVL type has a critical weight at which it can no longer land vertically. This was the main factor in the 2003-05 weight reduction effort, which had a knock-on effect on the subsequent development program.

The value of STOVL, at a national strategic level, was never assessed against the cost or performance penalties of producing Air Force and

---

replaced. (Ryberg 2002)

[49] The F/A-18E/F Super Hornet, with similar operating empty weight and installed thrust, is 66 feet long with a 44-foot wingspan.

Navy fighters that were derivatives of the STOVL design, but these were considerable. Two GE F414s would have provided equivalent thrust for far lower R&D cost and lower procurement cost[50]. The single engine weighed more than two F414s[51].

A non-STOVL design would have had a higher fineness ratio and lower transonic drag[52], without STOVL, the program would have had a shorter and simpler demonstration program, and the weight overruns of 2003-04 would have been more easily managed.

As for the value of STOVL: The Marine air combat element is primarily a support to Marine amphibious landing operations. It is almost impossible to imagine circumstances where such operations would require a supersonic, stealthy fighter aircraft but not Navy- or Air Force-unique support such as AEW&C and electronic attack.

Marine air power advocates have stressed the value of off-runway operations, but these had seldom been practiced in combat with the Harrier force[53]. The RAF had practiced off-base operations in various ways in Northern Europe in the Cold War[54] but no CONOPS had been established that delivered a high sustained sortie rate. The question of whether the F-35 would be able to operate away from hardened concrete surfaces even as freely as the Harrier[55] was never investigated.

---

[50] According to DoD contract announcements.

[51] F135 fact sheet published in 2008

[52] China's Shenyang J-35 and South Korea's KAI KF-21 are both in the F-35 class and show what the airplane might have looked like in the absence of a STOVL requirement.

[53] Marine Public Affairs documents show this happening once per major campaign.

[54] https://www.rafmuseum.org.uk/documents/research/RAF-Historical-Society-Journals/Journal-35A-Seminar-the-RAF-Harrier-Story.pdf

[55] The idea of flying out of fields or woodland hides was an appealing myth from the early days of STOVL and was quite impractical in practice. The last CONOPS practiced by RAF Germany envisaged the use of light industrial parks adjacent to straight stretches of road.

The JSF plan assumed that the application of new technology could reduce production and support costs compared with earlier combat aircraft. In the 1990s, manufacturing was undergoing a worldwide revolution, inspired by expanding global trade and the success of Japanese industry in automobiles and other markets. In the early 90s, pioneering organizations such as Boeing's Phantom Works focused on reducing production costs with maturing computer-aided engineering, technologies such as high-speed machining, large unitized structures, and "lean manufacturing" to reduce rework and increase productivity.

Attempts to reduce manufacturing cost, while incorporating both stealth and STOVL, led to serious weight gain early in the program. The failure to predict the actual weight was partly attributed to the complexity of the structural and systems design, with load paths and systems routed around the engine tunnel and the lift-fan bay.

Another cause of the weight gain was that the joints between the large unitized structures that were planned in the Concept Demonstration stage were themselves heavy. The program had to revert to more conventional construction, which proved difficult to produce to the tolerances demanded by stealth. For example, each set of wing skins and spars must be assembled, laser-mapped, then taken apart so that it can be shimmed to maintain a precise outer mold line.

The redesign was extensive, and the F-35 emerged from the weight crisis as three very different aircraft. (Fig. 2)[56] The OEW of the F-35B is ~2900 lbs. greater than the F-35A even though the STOVL powered-lift system adds 4000 lbs. to the weight, not including the complex door mechanisms. From this it can be calculated that the basic structure of the B is 10-15% lighter than that of the F-35A. This was achieved by paring down the size of the control surfaces, switching some bulkheads from Ti to Al and other measures. Conversely, the F-35C entered a weight spiral as the wing and tail

---

[56] JSF program briefs, author's collection

were enlarged to meet CV recovery requirements, and weighs 5500 lbs. more empty than the F-35A - 28% without the engine.

Reliance on new technology in logistics and prognostics - an extension of built-in testing – to deliver lower support costs proved ill-founded. Civilian logistics were improving quickly: Federal Express was familiar, and Amazon and eBay, along with e-commerce sites of established retailers such as Land's End, launched in 1994-95. A related part of the new industrial revolution was "just-in-time" procurement of parts and materials. The aircraft's prognostic systems would warn of a part about to fail, and the system would be preparing to ship it automatically to the air base before the jet landed.

A dynamic system such as an aircraft, it turns out, is too complex for a prognostic system based on prescriptive rules or lookup tables. More recent systems have used "big data" analysis to mine an actual base of operational data for signals of incipient failure.

As the only new fighter program in prospect for decades, the JSF program became the launch platform for new technologies that had been developed separately from it. The USAF had been working on the Joint Integrated Subsystems Technologies (J/IST) before JSF started: The goal was to improve reliability and reduce cost by combining the engine start, auxiliary and emergency power, and environmental control on a single turbine-compressor shaft.

An associated initiative was the "more electric airplane" where most of the airplane-wide hydraulic system would be replaced by electrical power distribution, including individual electro-hydraulic actuators for the primary flight controls.

Also baselined on JSF was a long-studied "big picture" cockpit with a single panoramic color digital display replacing the entire panel, combined with a sophisticated helmet-mounted display system (HMDS). This would provide the pilot with zero-light visibility, from an array of six infra-red sensors covering a sphere around the airplane.

Fig. 2 F-35 Weight Growth 2002-2005-Current

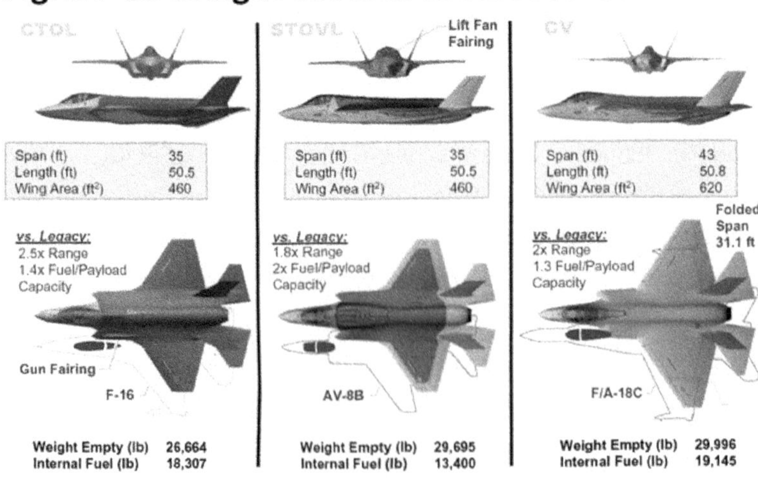

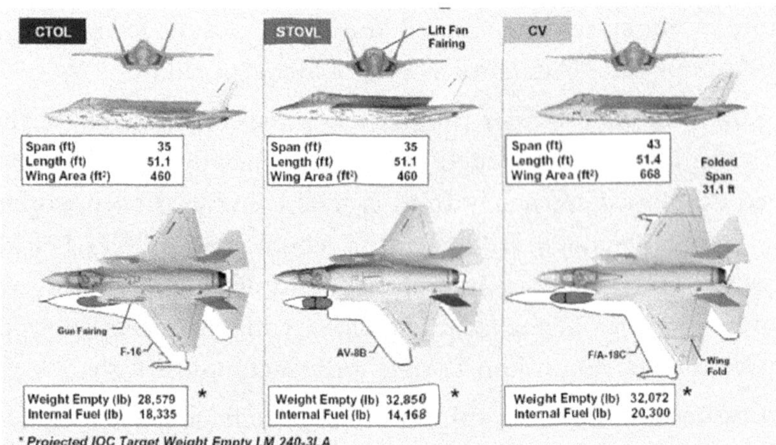

	F-35A CTOL	F-35B STOVL	F-35C CV
Length	51.4 ft / 15.67 m	51.2 ft / 15.61 m	51.5 ft / 15.7 m
Height	14.2 ft	14.1 ft	14.9 ft
Speed	Mach 1.6 (~1,200 mph)	Mach 1.6 (~1,200 mph)	Mach 1.6 (~1,200 mph)
Wingspan	35 ft / 10.67 m	35 ft / 10.67 m	43 ft / 13.11 m
Wing area	460 ft2 / 42.7 m2	460 ft2 / 42.7 m2	668 ft2 / 62.06 m2
Horizontal tail span	23 ft	22 ft	26 ft
Combat radius (internal fuel)	>590 nm / 1,093 km	>450 nm / 833 km	>600 n.mi / 1,111 km
Range (internal fuel)	>1,200 nm / 2,222 km	>900 nm / 1,667 km	>1,200 n.mi / 2,222 km
Internal fuel capacity	18,250 lb / 8278 kg	13,500 lb / 6,123.5 kg	19,750 lb / 8,958.5 kg
Weight empty	29,300 lb	32,000 lb	34,800 lb
Maximum weight	70,000 lb class	60,000 lb class	70,000 lb class
Max g-rating	9.0	7.0	7.5
Weapons payload	18,000 lb / 8,164.67 kg	15,000 lb / 6,803.89 kg	18,000 lb / 8,164.67 kg

The HMDS would replace the head-up display (which was physically incompatible, at the time, with the panoramic screen), cue the pilot to targets, and be able to be used to target weapons.

But these "pet rock" technologies would cause problems of their own. Classic hydraulic flight controls are self-cooling via their own circulating hydraulic fluid; electrohydraulic actuators needed a separate cooling circuit, and were large and bulky.

The HMDS has gone through multiple iterations of development, to solve problems such as providing the same boresight accuracy as a fixed HUD for precision tasks such as gunnery and carrier landing – and, ironically, technology has now evolved to a point where a fixed HUD and a big-screen display can be used together.

LAST SUPPER, BITTER DESSERT

When the major characteristics of the JSF program and air vehicle were being defined, in 1995-96, the world seemed to be entering a period of peace and stability anchored by the unipolar power of the United States. The Cold War had ended with the complete defeat of the Soviet Union: the loss of historically Russian territory as well as the breakup of the Warsaw Pact. China's post-Mao economic rise was in its early stages.

U.S. national security strategy was to be prepared for Iraq-style wars, but its strength far overmatched any likely adversary. A "two-MRC"-based (major regional conflict) became the default strategy, calling for changes to the military, such as the retirement of older equipment, that would deliver cost savings, but be non-traumatic.

The modernization of China's military, and the indigenization of Chinese defense technology, started after the Taiwan Strait crisis of 1995-96 and showed results in the early 2000s, but the West - preoccupied with the aftermath of the 9/11 attacks - was slow to recognize that development, so it put little pressure on the JSF program.

The disconnect was best symbolized by actions and events in 2008-11. Defense Secretary Robert Gates fired the Air Force's two top leaders in June 2008, frustrated because the service was seemingly resistant to buying as many MQ-9 UAVs (largely useless in peer conflict) as Gates wanted for the Middle East. In April 2009, Gates terminated the F-22 program and, later in the year, canceled the nascent project for a new strategic bomber.

Strongly supportive of the F-35 – which he characterized as being only a few years behind the F-22 and costing half as much - Gates in July 2009 declared his view that China would not have any stealth aircraft in 2020 and "a handful" in 2025. But at the end of 2010, China unveiled the Chengdu J-20 stealth fighter, and it was quickly apparent that it was a true prototype and not a technology demonstrator: today, it is estimated that more than 200 J-20s are in service and a carrier-based stealth fighter, the FC-31, is in flight test.

Systematic cyber-espionage against the defense establishment was recognized as early as 2008, but named only as the "Advanced Persistent Threat", even though Chinese military intelligence was known to be the source[57].

A 2008 study postulating that an F-35-based force would be vulnerable to long-range counter-air attacks in a China Sea scenario[58] drew an infuriated response from Lockheed Martin and the JSF Program Office[59]. The AirSea Battle concept for deterring China was controversial in 2011 and never fully implemented, despite evidence of China's ability to develop and field advanced technology.[60]

On the business side, the root-and-branch restructuring of the aerospace and defense industry following the 1993 "Last Supper" meeting and the launch of JSF went beyond expectations, and combined with other trends and pressures to restructure not only the defense industry, but its relationship to its Pentagon customer.

Companies that expected to retain prime status used merger and acquisition (M&A) aggressively, to absorb weaker primes, expand their markets (from aircraft into space, for example), establish themselves in long-tail sustainment business, and shed low-margin activity such as aerostructures and systems. (Fig. 3)[61]

---

[57] At a conference in 2008, a Lockheed Martin executive related that the company had investigated the security of small businesses linked to the F-35 contractor network, and found one where the person in charge of the network was also the receptionist.

[58] https://medium.com/war-is-boring/one-analyst-predicted-the-f-35s-s-dogfight-failure-50a942d0cf8a

[59] https://news.lockheedmartin.com/2008-09-19-Setting-the-Record-Straight-on-F-35

[60] "Too Little, Too Late", Sweetman and Fisher, Defense Technology International, April 2011

[61] "The US Defense Industrial Base, Past, Present and Future" – Barry Watts,

Conversely, companies that were not well positioned to survive raced to sell businesses to those expanding primes. (For example, General Dynamics sold off its missile business to Raytheon, and combat aircraft and space activities to Lockheed, while General Electric divested radar, flight control, space and other businesses to different buyers).

Fig. 3 Defense Consolidation 1993-2007

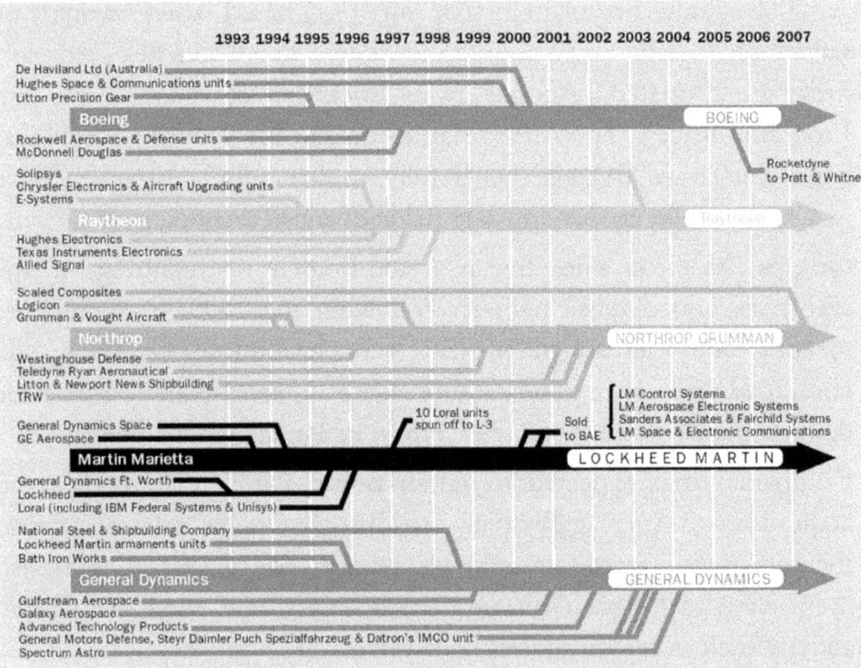

A third group of companies emerged as consolidators, acquiring first-tier suppliers and cast-off divisions, and forming them into brands with strong positions in certain niches. That process has continued into the present day with the formation of RTX and L3Harris.

The hottest management goal for U.S. business in the 1990s was established by General Electric CEO Jack Welch in the 1980s: to become among the leaders in every segment they were in, in order to

---

CSBA 2008

maximize growth, profits, and shareholder value. In the 2000s, shareholder value increasingly became an end in itself – a trend boosted by the fact that stock options in a strong economy were a growing part of executive compensation.

But starting in the 2000s, a number of major programs – of which the F-35 was one – started to overrun costs and suffer major problems. The Army cancelled its Comanche helicopter, its Future Combat System, and an advanced self-propelled gun. The Navy cut back its DDG-1000 stealth destroyer to three ships, while its Littoral Combat Ship program suffered delays and mechanical problems.

Pentagon leaders – notably the late SecDef Ashton Carter and Frank Kendall, his acquisition leader – developed a plan called Better Buying Power to drive costs down, through the leverage provided by the Pentagon's budget and its monopsony status.

The Pentagon focused increasingly on price when it picked the winners in major new programs, believing that since there were fewer of these, the government had the leverage to do so. The winning strategy was to propose a solution tailored exactly to the letter of the requirement at a "price to win" level, informed by detailed studies of what competitors were likely to bid.

The Pentagon encouraged primes to submit low-margin bids by leaving the intellectual property (IP) aspects of the program in their hands. The concession was not perceived as important by Congress and the public. Sustainment revenues in the early days of a program carry little weight in terms of shareholder value - after all, the program may be cut back or even cancelled - and become steadily more important as the program matures.

But IP rights become crucial as systems become digitally integrated, and less and less sustainment work can be done without the integrating contractor's permission. People have called these modern military aircraft "flying iPhones" but in fact "flying Tesla" may be a more apposite term.

The lesson of Better Buying Power for the remaining major primes was that margins on winning a new program were thin, and sometimes negative. The company leaders found it more profitable, and less risky, to defend existing business.

In this "fortress prime" world, defending existing business allows the primes to earn more from sustainment. At the same time, primes are showing increasing willingness to "no-bid" programs for which they are qualified, if they believe that the customer simply wants to increase price pressure on their favored candidate, or that a competitor will "buy in" with a low price[62]. And because the primes cover so many areas of business, they may still be able to take part in the program as first-tier subcontractors[63]. The superprimes' ability to no-bid further reduces the DoD's leverage and makes it harder to execute new programs.

At the same time, primes exploit their size and broad reach to squeeze suppliers to reduce their cost and margins, whether by recompeting their parts of the program or threatening to do so.

The narrow industrial base plus reliance on sustainment money makes cancellation/major truncation next to impossible. Other than one suspended $614 million fee in 2010, Lockheed Martin has not paid a single penalty for its performance.

The net result is that short of propaganda, jawboning and political pressure, the DoD has little leverage when it comes to controlling sustainment costs.

While a detailed study of U.S. national politics is beyond the scope of this study, the political environment in which the F-35 has been developed was very different from the 1960-90 period, when defense acquisition decisions were major national issues, politically and

---

[62] Examples of this include Northrop Grumman's exit from a Navy unmanned air vehicle program, and Lockheed Martin's withdrawal from an agreement with Airbus to offer an alternative tanker.

[63] For instance, it is possible that NGC has agreed with Lockheed Martin or Boeing to collaborate on NGAD.

publicly controversial, and drew focused attention from the executive and legislative branches.

The 1992-2000 Clinton administration had promised a "peace dividend" and had to balance its desire to cut defense spending with the need to retain a path to renewing the force, including the TacAir fleet, in the future. The JSF plan was ideal, because it offered a workable replacement plan, but would require relatively little funding – only a demonstration program – for the duration of a second term.

Defense policy in the Bush administration of 2000-2008 was dominated by the 9/11 attacks, the invasion or Iraq and the warfare in Afghanistan and Iraq that followed. There was almost zero interest, at top levels, in any new weapons not usable for close air support or tactical intelligence, surveillance and reconnaissance. The F 35 attracted little attention and was not the subject of controversy until the above-mentioned wargame story broke in September 2008.

In a departure from normal procedure, the Obama administration of 2008-2016 retained SecDef Bob Gates - who, as noted above, doubled down on the F-35 in 2008-09. Then, from Gates's departure in June 2011) through the unserious Trump regime, and until the incumbent at the time of writing, no SecDef served for two years.

The War on Terror monopolized the attention of Congress and the media, as far as defense was concerned. Unlike earlier troubled defense programs[64], the F-35 was the subject of very little critical reporting, whether in general or specialist media, and while Congress required regular reports on the F-35 from the Government Accountability Office, these seldom resulted in legislative action, beyond requirements for more reports.

[64] The B-2 and V-22 programs, in particular, received far more critical coverage than the F-35.

ONE BIG TOXIC FAMILY

The F-35 program was not only massive, but faced the challenge of meeting a complex requirement, requiring solutions to new technological problems, in a changing environment in terms of national strategic policies, industrial development, and politics. But its management structure was modelled on smaller, conventional Pentagon programs that reported directly to service operators. The project leadership rotated, comprising a two-star director and a one-star deputy serving four years, two in each position, supported mainly by senior executive service staff.

When this structure was established, the industry's reconstruction was under way, but the "fortress prime" culture had yet to emerge. A more collegial culture was expected.

As a joint program, JPO did not report to an operational service customer. The Air Force was the largest buyer, but during the Global War on Terror era, which included the firing of its senior leaders, its influence was at its nadir. The contracting agency was the Navy.

Nominally, the JPO reported to the Under Secretary of Defense for Acquisition, Technology, and Logistics[65] in the Office of the Secretary of Defense (OSD). But in the post-9/11 era, OSD did not have bandwidth to manage the program in detail, and, as noted above, successive SecDefs either had other priorities, were actively supportive, or were not in office long.

There was no supervisory board or equivalent body that had the authority, accountability, and independence that would have been needed to strengthen OSD control over the program. There is a JSF Executive Steering Board (JESB), but it is primarily a window for international customers – "a forum for discussions, consultations and decisions", and normally has a one- or two-day half-yearly meeting[66]. GAO and DOT&E provided oversight, but wielded no authority.

---

[65] USD(AT&L), known popularly as the "procurement czar"

Conversely, 1990s mergers and acquisitions made the contractors larger and more powerful. The JSF Program Office became the object of "regulatory capture"[67]– a process in which a government agency begins to identify its aims as congruent with those of private institutions - and at times seemed to be as engaged in marketing efforts as the contractors were, joining them to minimize problems. For example, the JPO, Pratt & Whitney were united behind the successful campaign to remove General Electric's F136 engine from the program.

The JPO routinely pushed back against GAO, the Director of Operational Test & Evaluation, and others who challenged the feasibility of the schedule, whether in Congress or the media. This was congruent with the primes' interest in defending the program.

Dysfunctional management revealed itself in three main ways: **optimistic and infeasible responses** to major unexpected difficulties; **a lack of candor** about at least two major issues; and **a marketing-based communications strategy and culture** that was propagandistic and impeded public understanding of the program's problems.

Symptom 1: Responses To Sequential Crises

By 2007-2008, it was clear from a series of schedule slippages that the program was not effectively managing its way through the inevitable engineering difficulties. These slippages continued into 2010, and were accompanied by briefings that were clearly misleading: given the gap between PowerPoint briefings and the reality, with events predicted only months in the future not occurring until much later, the briefers were either misinformed, or disingenuous (Fig 4).

---

[66] https://www.state.gov/wp-content/uploads/2019/02/06-1231-Multilateral-Defense-JSF.pdf, Sec 4

[67] https://www.brookings.edu/articles/what-is-regulatory-capture/

Fig. 4 F-35 Schedules 2001-2008-2010

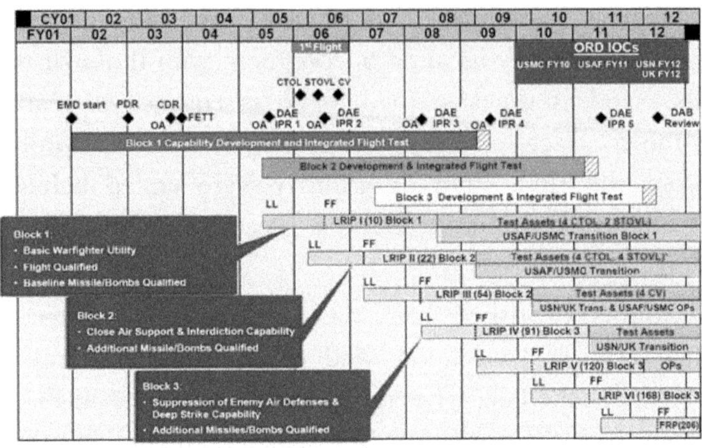

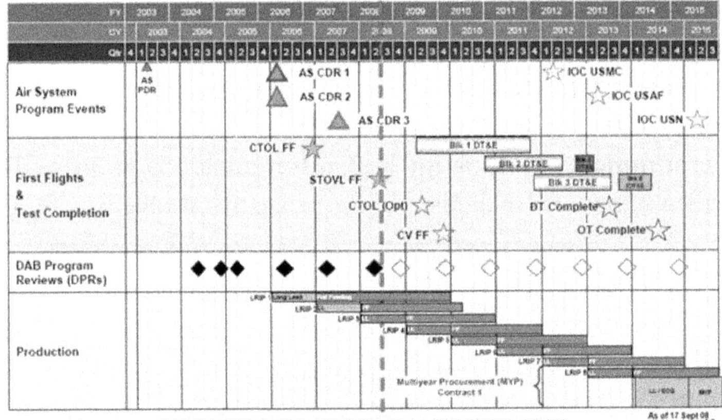

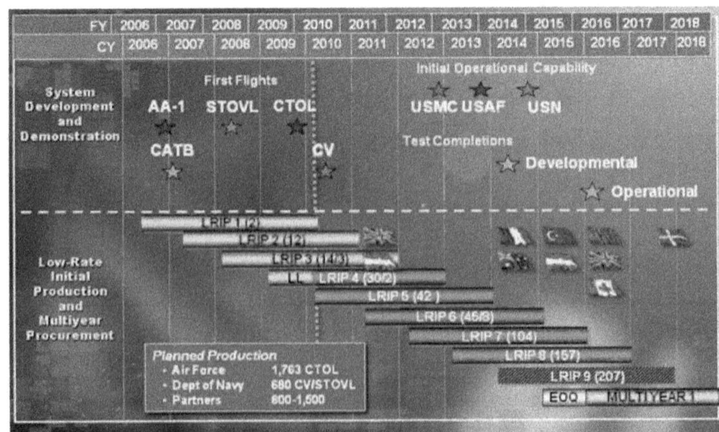

A pattern emerged that became clearly identifiable later in the 2010s. Given the primes' focus on defending the program, a “fail ure is not an option" mindset governed decision-making, resulting in a repeated cycle of events.

Crisis: A major problem threatened to stall the program's progress or even lead to termination.

"Get well": To minimize the impact of the problem on the cost and schedule, program leadership would mandate a solution that was schedule-driven and based on optimistic assumptions.

Next crisis: The solution missed its cost and schedule targets and/or drew attention and resources from other issues, often becoming an aggravating or causative factor in the next problem[68].

Several of these "rolling crisis" cycles can be identified:

1999-2001 "It won't fly"

Crisis: As source selection approaches in 2000, Boeing's design proves incapable of a vertical landing and the lift-fan system of Lockheed Martin's X-35 is unreliable, raising the possibility that neither will complete a STOVL demo.

"Get well": Rather than re-evaluating the premise of the project, the fact that the X-35 does make it through its tests is treated as validation.

Next crisis: The "success" of Mission X[69] obscures the fact that the X-35 is smaller than the operational design (lacking space for weapon bays), that the Preferred Weapon System Concept is immature, and that the program involves considerable risk.

---

[68] This story arc will be familiar to those who remember the Burl Ives song "I Know An Old Lady Who Swallowed A Fly".

[69] Mission X involves a short take-off, acceleration to supersonic speed and a vertical landing.

2003-2005 Weight Overrun

Crisis: As critical design review approaches in 2003, it is discovered that the F-35B is 3,300 lb. overweight and will be incapable of vertical landing. (Earlier in 2003, it was believed that the jet had margin to spare[70].)

"Get well": In 2004, it is announced that the weight improvement program has succeeded and that the project will slip by only 12 months, even though the weight reduction includes substantial change to the outer mold line and much less commonality across the three versions.

Next crisis: The unrealistic schedule manifests itself in delays in manufacturing the redesigned aircraft for the flight test program.

2008-2010 Delivery Delays

Crisis: With many design changes being implemented concurrently across three variants, development aircraft fall months behind schedule in manufacture.

"Get well": Program leadership eliminates sorties from the flight-test program, while prioritizing formal delivery and first flights for development aircraft that are not ready to join the test program without months of rework.

Next crisis: As flight testing falls behind schedule, discoveries that should have been made in time for fixes to be incorporated very early in production are made later, when more aircraft are on the line.

2010-2013 Technical Challenges

Crisis: With production approaching 40 aircraft per year, there are major unresolved issues at the flight-sciences level, and with key systems such as the HMDS. It becomes clear that the JPO has

[70] In a 2003 interview, LM program manager Tom Burbage said that favorable weight projections were one reason for the switch to a heavier gun system.

both underestimated the number of test sorties and events required and overestimated the attainable pace of testing.

"Get well": The program director is fired, and new leadership installed. Ultimately, the DoD is forced to extend the SDD schedule by three years, but to avoid either a drastic production slowdown or the visible accumulation of hundreds of non-operational airplanes, two interim operational standards (F-35B Block 2B and F-35A Block 3i) are adopted.

Next crisis: The need to develop, test and de-bug 2B and 3i puts more pressure on the 3F schedule, but hardware issues have pulled resources away from software.

2013 - 2017– Mounting software problems

Crisis: Development of the avionics hardware and software threatens further delay to IOC.

"Get well": More coders are hired, and a rapid-fire sequence of S/W standards is established. A level of bugginess is accepted in 3F.

Next crisis: With multiple operational standards, the growing fleet imposes a support problem - and it is realized that Autonomic Logistics Information System (ALIS) has been inadequately developed and is seriously flawed.

2014-Ongoing - Support issues

Crisis: As soon as F-35s hit Air Force squadrons, there are complaints that F-35 operations are robbing first-line units of experienced personnel.[71]

"Get well"; Trust is placed in the elite coders of Kessel Run, an Air Force-funded software workshop, to replace ALIS with Odin, a different system making more use of data analysis and machine learning.

---

[71] F-16 unit commander, speaking under Chatham House Rules at a 2014 conference in London

Next crisis: The program under-invests in 2013-15 in ground-based software and associated hardware – reprogramming labs and ALIS, for instance - contributing to test delays and support problems, and the future Block 4.1 becomes a set of fixes to 3F, pushing actual system improvements into 4.2.

2018-Ongoing – Block 4 Issues

Crisis: Concern mounts that the 4.1/4.2/TR3 program cannot be executed as planned. L3Harris, selected after a recompete to build a new Integrated Core Processor, is falling behind schedule. The new processor requires new software.

"Get well": The JPO first talks (2018) about a quick turn deployment of many software blocks under the Continuous Capability and Development Delivery (C2D2) rubric, but this proves unmanageable. Block 4 expands into a ~$16.5 billion program in its own right, and a big driver of unacceptable sustainment costs. Delay is not an option because TR-3 avionics are installed from FY21 aircraft onward.

Next crisis: Block 4/C2D2 collapses after software fails to overcome problems with hastily developed and defective hardware, resulting in a two-year-plus halt in the delivery of combat-capable aircraft. The original schedule for delivering 80-plus modifications and capabilities under Block 4 is abandoned, and development of a new plan starts.

2022-Ongoing -Thermal and Power

Crisis: Long-running "in-background" thermal management issue has been persistently understated and results in speed restrictions – higher speeds and lower altitudes cause hotter environments. It is disclosed in September 2021 that thermal management is inadequate for Block 4, which uses more power than Block 3.

"Get well": Timing and the need for compatibility across USAF, DoN and International users preclude all options other than a sole-source engine upgrade, which does nothing for range or transonic acceleration issues, along with a new Power & Thermal Management System.

Next crisis: Mandatory bills for international users surge again - costs for modifications were estimated at >$20 m unit before the engine bills (~$15m?) came in.

Symptom 2: Absence Of Candor And Denial Of Problems

Two major issues were systematically downplayed by program leaders, and one, additionally, by senior officers. The first of these to be reported was inadequate thermal management capacity.

A tactical fighter generates waste heat in a tightly packed space, from avionics, electrical systems, and from the exterior of the engine. On a conventional aircraft, much of this heat is lost to outside air, either directly through venting, via the environmental control system, or through the skin. This is harder to do on a stealth aircraft because it creates hot-spots that can be detected by infrared sensors.

In the design of the F-35, heat would be removed by coolant circuits built into the avionics and either dumped into the fuel via heat exchangers, dissipating the energy overboard as fuel was burned, or via heat exchangers in the engine fan duct.

DOT&E reported as early as 2004 that this could be a problem. The system could cool the aircraft at high altitude and with full tanks, but fuel temperature would rise continuously towards safety limits at lower altitudes, or at the end of the mission when less fuel was on board to absorb the heat within fuel-temperature limits.

There was no single cause for the "thermal deficit", but it appears both that systems were shedding more heat than predicted and that the novel and complex power and thermal management system (Fig.5) had less capacity than expected. One unique source of heat was the electrohydraulic

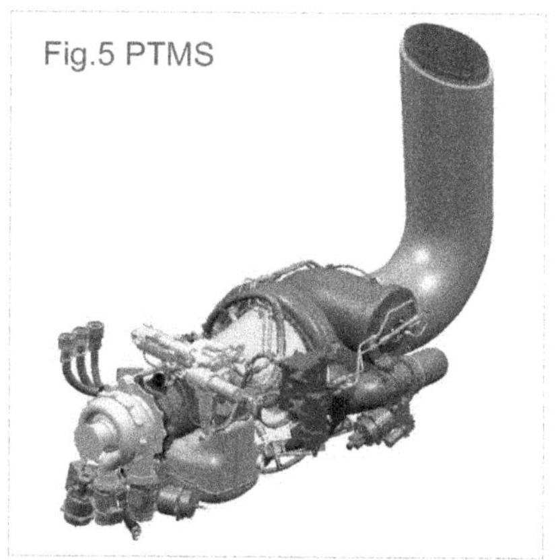
Fig.5 PTMS

actuation of the flight controls system; as advocates of hydraulic systems observed, the movement of fluid throughout the system cooled the actuators to the same level, but the EHAs required their own liquid cooling connections to the PTMS.

In public, the JPO and contractors played the issue down, insisting in the late 2000s that a more efficient fuel pump would solve the problem. The problem received renewed public attention in late 2014 when Luke AFB's public affairs office announced that its ground crews were painting tankers white to keep fuel cooler and alleviate problems with newly arrived F-35s; the JSF PR organization immediately responded by dismissing the problem completely and insisting that "This is not an F-35 issue; there are no special restrictions on the F-35 related to fuel temperature."[72]

The thermal issues have persisted, and – in mid-2024 – are severe enough that it is now considered that some planned Block 4 changes cannot be accommodated until the redesigned engine core and a new PTMS are available, costing many billions of dollars in R&D and retrofits.

Another major problem emerged at the end of 2009, specific to the F-35B. The U.S. Marine Corps CONOPS for the F-35B assumed the use of STOVL capability both aboard ships and from improvised bases ashore, to support the service's amphibious combined-arms mission. In those operations, LHA/LHD ships are needed to carry troops, weapons, helicopters and landing craft and normally carry a six-aircraft fighter detachment.

If the operation calls for more F-35s they must be accommodated on land, and the F-35B was designed to use short runways and improvised road bases, taking off with a 550-foot ground roll and landing vertically. But VL turned out to be impossible on normal runway surfaces.

[72] https://breakingdefense.com/2014/12/the-tale-of-the-f-35-and-hot-jet-fuel/

A December 2009 report from the Naval Facilities Engineering Command (NavFac)[73] disclosed that the main engine exhaust from an F-35B "will melt the top surface of asphalt pavements, and is likely to spall the surface of standard airfield concrete pavements on the first VL." Spalling in concrete occurs when subsurface water boils, causing the surface to break into flakes. To perform a safe vertical landing outside a steel ship deck, the F-35 would need a 100 x 100-foot landing pad constructed from reinforced, high-temperature concrete, NavFac recommended.

Lockheed Martin and the Marines dismissed the specifications as based on worst-case assessments and old data. The company said that it had conducted extensive ground-environment tests in January 2010. "Results indicate that the difference between F-35B main-engine exhaust temperature and that of the AV-8B is very small," the program office told the media, "and is not anticipated to require any significant CONOPS changes."[74] In March 2010, then-Marine Commandant Gen. James Conway told DoD Buzz that the JSF exhaust "at 1,500 degrees is just 18 degrees hotter than a Harrier."[75]

This was not the case: NavFac's assessment had been correct. Multiple high-temperature VL pads have been constructed at F-35 bases in the U.S. and UK.[76] The Royal Navy was also apparently unaware of the exhaust-heat issue. It was not until May 2012 - after its flirtation with converting its carriers to catapult/arrest operations - that the RN initiated a project to develop a thermal metal spray system to coat the decks of its aircraft carriers[77].

To this day, the F-35B has seldom if ever been observed to perform a VL other than on a steel ship deck or a specially built landing pad.

---

[73] https://www.wbdg.org/FFC/NAVFAC/INTCRIT/ARCHIVES/fy10_01.pdf

[74] Defense Technology International, October 2011

[75] https://www.military.com/dodbuzz/2010/03/26/jsf-not-too-hot-for-carriers

[76] "F-35 jets use new vertical landing pads at RAF Marham for the first time", MoD News, July 25, 2018. The pads can also be easily located on Google Earth.

[77] https://www.ddcoatings.co.uk/1275/new-deck-coating-hms-queen-

The aircraft has hovered at air shows, but at least 100 feet above the ground. Marine "off-base" exercises have used the aircraft in STOL mode - where the exhaust is oblique to the ground, and constantly moving - but on strips no less than 6,000 feet long, that could accommodate many conventional fighters.[78]

Symptom 3: A Propagandistic Communications Culture

Misleading rhetoric was integral to a communications strategy that was qualitatively different from earlier programs. Total honesty is not expected in politics or advertising. Accomplishments are trumpeted; problems are allowed to leak out, accompanied by responses that minimize the difficulties and offer optimistic promises of quick and cheap solutions. In most industries, too, there is a cultural aversion to "knocking copy" that flat-out disparages the competition, and it is seldom customary to criticize the customer's judgment.

Driven by the need to protect the program at all costs, F-35 communications strategists departed from these norms, and finding no negative consequences, became steadily more extreme.

Government watchdog groups and organizations such as the GAO, DOT&E and the Joint Estimating Team (a cross-service group) were criticized for working on old data, and ignoring the JSF program's more recent progress[79]; or for using earlier programs as the baseline for JSF cost projections, when the program asserted that it had learned from those programs and was more efficient. Subsequent events generally proved the critics right[80]. At one point, a paid F-35 advocate asserted that the "testing bureaucracy" was deliberately slowing the program down in their financial self-interest.[81]

---

elizabeth-aircraft-carrier

[78] https://www.thedrive.com/the-war-zone/f-35b-just-touched-down-on-the-old-pacific-coast-highway

[79] They had no sources of data other than the JPO and the contractors

[80] "Inflated F-35 Cost Estimates Ignore Reality", Lexington Institute, October 26, 2009). Loren Thompson's Lexington Institute was hired to project the program's message.

The campaign to secure the cancellation of General Electric's F136 alternate engine marked an early deployment of complete falsehood. P&W and its representatives repeatedly asserted that P&W had won multiple competitions to power the F-35, and that the F136 program was a political creation. No competition had taken place, as was confirmed by the public record[82]; the alternate engine had been part of the program since 1996.

As the program entered its third crisis cycle, in 2008, public briefings became divorced from reality. By September 2009, the flight test program was the slowest of its kind in history, in terms of test aircraft being delivered and hours and flights accrued. Nevertheless, the project's leaders were expressing public confidence that, within a year, the test program would be setting record speed levels with 150 productive sorties per month. This never happened because aircraft were not delivered on time: in a media visit in April 2009, a small area at the end of the assembly line was tightly packed with aircraft not ready for delivery, while the flight-line barns contained F-35s that had nominally been delivered but that required modification before they could join the flight-test program.

The F-35 was exclusively presented as superior to all other fighters, by a massive margin. It was stated that the F-35 was "at least 400 percent more effective in air-to-air combat capability than the best fighters currently available in the international market" and that "advanced stealth and sensor fusion allow the F-35 pilot to see, target and destroy the adversary and strategic targets in a very high surface-to-air threat scenario, and deal with air threats intent on denying access -- all before the F-35 is ever detected."[83]

---

[81] https://www.lexingtoninstitute.org/pentagon-slow-roll-of-f-35-fighter-hurts-budget-trade-balance-burdensharing/

[82] Because the engine is a complex system and critical to performance and safety, it was planned from the outset to develop two engine types for the F-35. However, GE would follow P&W by some years so as to be ready for production rather than development.

[83] https://news.lockheedmartin.com/2008-09-19-Setting-the-Record-Straight-

From 2009 onwards, no public material departed from the official line, which was that the F-35 outclassed all other aircraft in every mission (with the exception of the F-22 in the air-dominance mission), while costing less to acquire and sustain[84]. Sustainment costs were predicted to be lower than the F-16.

In 2008, Norway was seen to be wobbling towards possible collaboration with Sweden on Gripen. The nation was persuaded to conduct an evaluation, which concluded that Gripen would be far more expensive than JSF, on the basis of projected lifetime support costs. The exercise was successful enough to dissuade Boeing from taking an aggressive line to promote an improved F/A-18 against F-35C: "We are concerned that we will be publicly repudiated."[85]

From 2004 onward, LM ingeniously used the "fifth-generation" tag[86] to promote the F-35. Most of its competitors responded by arguing the merits of "4gen" or "4gen-plus", thereby sounding defensive, rather than observing that LO was one aspect of fighter capability, had its own costs and was not yet operational[87].

The JSF was the first defense program of the Internet era. Its inception coincided with the integration of PowerPoint into the basic Microsoft Office platform, and it grew up alongside that controversial tool, known for its power to confuse as well as to communicate[88]. As the project continued and the debate became more intense, new media emerged: blogs attached to traditional media, with open comment sections, and independent message and discussion forums. When these discussed the F-35 program, the invariable result was an influx of intensely pro-F-35 commenters who

---

on-F-35

[84] In 2024, nobody has a definitive prediction of the F-35's mature sustainment cost.

[85] Boeing source to author, 2011

[86] Originally used by Russian industry.

[87] Notably, Dassault did not play this game and the Rafale became the second most commercially successful fighter of the 2010s-2020s, behind the F-35.

[88] https://www.edwardtufte.com/tufte/powerpoint

rejected any criticism of the program and accused critics of being incompetent, biased, or even being paid agents.

There is some evidence of direct contractor involvement in this activity, and some pro-JSF keyboard warriors are known to have been government or industry employees, but the nature of interactive media at the time, with all contributors using pseudonyms and very simple sign-up procedures, lent itself to exploitation by "reputation management" companies working on contract.

As the Internet grew, traditional media lost business. The defense trade media suffered from the merger mania, as advertising budgets were combined, page counts shrank, and there was less room for long and deeply researched stories.

Secrecy played an important role. Immediately after the end of the Cold War, there was a period of relative candor concerning stealth technology; at a conceptual level it could be discussed openly in some detail. This changed in the 2000s, and stealth again became mysterious. This made it easier to frame low-observables technology as "game changing" – a phrase that, according to Google's nGram, rocketed from near-non-existence to universality between 1995 and 2010.

With the trade media shrinking, think-tanks, particularly in Washington D.C., remained major producers of long-form writing on defense issues. But Washington think-tanks in particular had been established by wealthy power centers as an offset to academia, seen as too left-liberal in the Vietnam era and later. Defense think-tanks were and are largely sponsored by industry, which can and does directly commission reports that support its views.

Between the F-35's cult-like following, sponsored think-tanks and a relatively impoverished independent media, the program enjoyed an easy ride despite schedule slips and budget overruns that in earlier years would have ensured it a very rough ride.

Throughout the program, there was an intense lack of introspection or retroflection. Apart from deputy program manager MG Chris Bogdan's lambasting of Lockheed Martin at the 2012 Air Force Association convention[89], and Air Force secretary Frank Kendall's characterization of the program in 2023 as "acquisition malpractice"[90], most of the lessons learned have been swept under the rug. Even an extensive series of papers presented at an American Institute of Aeronautics and Astronautics forum in 2018[91] largely avoids any discussion of the decisions that led to the program's troubles.

A history of the project by Tom Burbage[92], who headed the program at Lockheed Martin for some 15 years, acknowledges few if any errors, although Burbage does point to the decision to pull resources from software during the 2003-2004 weight crisis. It does devote considerable space to the program's struggles against "uninformed" critics – sustaining the F-35's lethal mission of shooting the messenger.

One final point, minor, perhaps, but symbolic. Since the start of the program, Lockheed Martin and the JPO have misstated the F-35's maximum speed, stating that it is Mach 1.6 and 1,200 mph. But as anyone in the business should know, Mach 1.6 = 1,200 mph at sea level. At the troposphere altitudes where most fighter aircraft can exceed Mach 1 (30,000 feet and above), Mach 1.6 = 1,060 mph.

---

89 F-35 Program's Relationship With Lockheed 'Worst I've Ever Seen,' Breaking Defense, September 17, 2012

90 "US Air Force wants to avoid F-35 mistakes on sixth-gen fighter": Defense News, May 22, 2023

91 "The F-35 Lightning II – From Concept to Cockpit", Jeffrey W. Hamstra, ed; AIAA 2019

92 "F-35: The Inside Story of the Lightning II" by Tom Burbage, Betsy Clark, Adrian Pitman, and David Poyer, published by Skyhorse Books, publisher of RFK Jr's anti-vaxx books and the well-known children's story "Glitterbutt The Farting Unicorn."

BREAKS IN THE LEVEE

Around 2010, the upper levels of the Pentagon realized that the F-35 program was failing at the most basic level. But by then the fighter fleet was aging, hostilities continued in the Middle East, the only other fighter in production for the U.S. services was the Super Hornet, and the growing threat from China was being recognized. The Pentagon elected to fix the program with new management.

Defense Secretary Gates had accepted the contractor's assurances in 2009 that the program was running smoothly, but a key change was the appointment in April 2009 of a new USD(AT&L) "acquisition czar", Ashton Carter, to replace John Young, who had gone out of his way to criticize JET and other independent estimators. Carter's investigations showed problems.

"I called the contractor into my office to discuss the program on a Saturday morning – a clear signal of my annoyance," Carter recalled later[93]. "Seeing his nonchalance about cost and schedule overruns, I walked out of the meeting." Carter and Gates then fired JPO director Maj Gen David Heinz and appointed Vice Adm Dave Venlet with an assignment to re-baseline the schedule. At the same time, Carter placed the F-35B "on probation" because of numerous problems, and in October the UK announced its intention to abandon the F-35B and modify its new carriers with catapults and arrester gear.

Eventually it took three years to even rebaseline the schedule – but by this time, the consequences of terminating the program became much more severe.

Hundreds of aircraft were on order from USAF, DoN and export customers, and the first export aircraft had been delivered. Moreover, there was rising tension with both China and Russia, and both were

---

[93] https://www.defenseone.com/ideas/2019/07/how-we-tamed-f-35s-spiraling-costs-and-created-model-controlling-waste/158344/

apparently making technological progress, both with their own stealth aircraft and counter-stealth systems[94].

No U.S. stealth combat aircraft other than the F-35 was being developed, except for the very different Long Range Strike Bomber. Delaying the program at that point was close to unthinkable – but hints of an alternative emerged in 2015.

In February 2015, Ash Carter's successor, Frank Kendall, announced the Aerospace Innovation Initiative to develop a new fighter demonstrator, via a specially established office within DARPA.[95]

Air Combat Command vice-commander MG Jerry Harris mentioned at a London conference in November 2015 that the USAF wanted to reduce the pace of its F-35 buys until the TR3/Block 4 version was ready, and was looking at ordering more advanced F-15s based on the latest version then being developed with Saudi funding. One concern was the labor and training involved in support, which would be a major problem if the USAF inducted large numbers of Block 3 aircraft[96].

In April 2016, Deputy Chief of Staff for Strategic Plans and Requirements Lt Gen Mike Holmes announced the results of an Air Superiority 2030 study, calling for a high-speed, long-range Penetrating Counter Air combat aircraft optimized for operations in the Western Pacific. Later known as a key part of the Next Generation Air Dominance (NGAD) program, this was the first new tactical combat aircraft to be proposed within the F-35 production timeline. Holmes and other leaders started talking, too, about a "new Century series" approach for faster development of new aircraft.

---

[94] "Great Wall", Aviation Week, November 17, 2014; "Cloak And Dagger", Aviation Week, September 2, 2013

[95] "Kendall unveils 6th generation strategy", Defense News Feb 1, 2015

[96] Harris disclosed this at the 2015 International Fighter Conference in London, under Chatham House rules which prevented him from being identified. This made it easier for the DoD to protect the F-35 by denying any such plans.

In October 2021, the USAF released a request for information on an Advanced Tactical Trainer (ATT) for lead-in fighter training, adversary air operations and, possibly, fighter operations in low-threat areas. The move was in part a response to concerns that the F-35's high operating cost would constrict the USAF's graduate-to-squadron pipeline as more were delivered and as F-16s left the force[97].

The U.S. Navy also launched studies of a follow-on aircraft, ostensibly to replace the F/A/-18E/F fleet as it ages out in the mid-2030s.

The UK performed a reversal of course after its 2015 Strategic Defence and Security Review, which reaffirmed its commitment to buying 138 F-35s and made no reference to a future combat aircraft program. This still seemed to be policy a year later. But within less than two years, the UK and Italy had agreed on a Future Combat Air Systems project with the Tempest full-scale demonstrator as its centerpiece, and with continued improvement of the Typhoon as part of its strategy.

In July 2022, in a major break from the Cold War pattern, Japan announced that it was joining the Anglo-Italian effort, now called Global Combat Aircraft Program (GCAP).

The reasons for the change in UK and Japanese policy have not been discussed publicly, but the author's view is that sovereignty is an important factor.

British defense minister Paul Drayson asserted in 2006 that the U.K. might exit the program if not given access to the source code to the aircraft, or the ability to generate mission data files – including adversary electronic order of battle information – under its own control.. As preparations continued for the introduction of the F-35 to British service, it became clear that the U.S. would remain

[97] https://www.defensenews.com/air/2021/12/01/with-t-7-on-the-way-why-is-acc-eyeing-a-new-trainer/

inflexible in the control of program information – it was announced in late 2009 that all programming would be under U.S. control.

As a stealth aircraft, the F-35 is subject to burdensome and costly Special Access Program security rules, defined by the DoD. Export customers must supply Government SAP Security Officers (GSSOs), approved by the U.S. and reporting to a U.S. Country Security Manager. One reason for the loss of a British F-35B in November 2021 was that the GSSOs required the use of inlet covers whenever the aircraft were on deck, and a contributing factor - crew fatigue aboard the carrier Queen Elizabeth - was linked to the GSSO's preventing the British ship's deck from being used for recreation.[98] But long before this, U.S.-imposed rules governed the creation of facilities at RAF Marham and onboard the carriers.

Another pain point in the U.S.-U.K. relationship over F-35 has been the integration of weapons. The U.K. has placed a high priority on its "complex weapons" sector and has a published goal of getting two weapons – the air-to-ground, high-precision SPEAR 3 and the long-range Meteor air-to-air missile – fully integrated on F-35. Even before the collapse of the Block 4 program, there was no firm schedule for this effort. British defense analysts note that the GBU-53/B StormBreaker glide bomb and AIM-120D air-to-air missile, rivals to SPEAR 3 and Meteor, are both made by F-35 team member RTX.

In the case of Japan, the country's Ministry of Defense had made it very clear in the process of planning its F-X next-generation fighter project that the "right to modify" was of paramount importance. The U.S. bid to support co-development took scant account of this concern.

The impact of the above on U.S. defense policy and planning has been limited since the 2016 election by the dysfunction in U.S. politics. Short-tenure SecDefs, a series of unqualified individuals in

[98] DSA investigation report, 2023

the Trump administration, and Congress preoccupied with national politics and struggles with opposition parties, have pushed acquisition policy to the sidelines. In this power vacuum, lobbyists defending established programs can and do dominate the picture.

A REAL LIVE NEPHEW OF MY UNCLE SAM

Despite problems, overruns and delays, the F-35 has been a success on the export market. Unsurprisingly, people point to this as evidence that the system is superior to its competitors in capability and cost, and that critics who point to its disadvantages are wrong. But even the most transparent evaluations are subject to outside influence.

The F-35 is an effective aircraft in many missions; the principal U.S. issue - that the F-35's late arrival has derailed the recapitalization of Air Force TacAir - does not apply to export customers who are getting the aircraft on a timescale of their own choosing. The U.S. has a strong reputation as a supplier of defense equipment, and customers likely believe that despite the project's troubles today or in the near future, they will be fixed by the time their aircraft arrive.

But it is naïve in the extreme for anyone to think that it does not matter which country a nation chooses to supply what in most cases is its most expensive and important weapon system, or that the U.S. Government is sitting on its hands and allowing some kind of free market to take its course.

The U.S. has always put pressure behind defense exports, but the position of the F-35 program is unique.

First, outside fixed-wing combat aircraft, the U.S. position today is not as dominant as it used to be. Non-U.S. companies are relatively stronger in airlift and tanker aircraft, helicopters, and national security space than they were 20 years ago. The DoD is now developing warships based on European designs, and Asian and European suppliers outperform U.S. companies in major land systems. The F-35 is the nation's leading defense export product.

Second, the economic benefits that the U.S. derives from F-35 exports are greater than normal. International partner deliveries were concentrated in the TR-2/Block 3 production lots, avoiding costly fluctuations in production rate in the years when the U.S. Air Force reduced its offtake, waiting for TR-3/Block 4. (In September 2013, it was stated that more than half the planned 2014-20 ramp-up in F-35 production was supported by exports[99].)

Third and most important, the nature of the F-35, as a software-heavy, networked, high-security system, changes the relationship between the customer's military and the U.S. In coalition and alliance training or operations, U.S. and partner F-35s are closely interoperable and almost interchangeable. Even an ally developing its own signals intelligence and incorporating results into mission data files can only do so in a U.S.-controlled facility, while some operational data from users is logged through the ALIS sustainment system or its successor.

Conversely, to a greater extent than most aircraft, the F-35 is not independently usable without active U.S. support. Whether the system incorporates a U.S.-accessible "kill switch" is another issue, but a defense analyst and observer Francis Tusa has noted: "I won't even attempt to go into the 'kill switch' debate – that several Middle East nations say that there is such is enough to leave it with."[100]

The result is that U.S. government and most of industry are in lockstep behind F-35, whereas in the past the F-16 and F/A-18 were rivals, respectively supported by the U.S. Air Force and Navy, and the government had to be even-handed between them. Selling the F-35 is a whole-of-government campaign involving the Departments of Defense and State.

The U.S. government has also been able to treat each target nation individually. Because of the high level of classification applied to the F-35, prospective F-35 buyers are limited even in their informal contacts with other nations in the market.

---

99 "Seoul Survivor", Aviation Week, September 30, 2013

100 RAeS Aerospace Magazine, January 2024

Nations looking for fighters are under two types of pressure. On the diplomatic side, the U.S. can stress to the potential customer that the U.S. regards interoperability as an important military advantage, and will give preference to allies who stand "shoulder to shoulder" with U.S. forces. This is particularly influential against the background of events such as the Ukraine war, given the United States' unique ability to supply munitions and other materiel in a crisis.

This pressure is candidly described in one of the Wikileaks cables, covering a campaign to prevent Norway from entering a joint development effort with Sweden on the JAS 39E. "We couldn't let stand the view that the choice didn't matter for the relationship", a U.S. official wrote, "We opted for 'choosing the JSF will maximize the relationship' as our main public line. In private, we were much more forceful."[101].

The importance of professional military links with the U.S. cannot be overestimated. Large-scale exports of F-16s, F/A-18s and F-15s started in the early 1980s, and by the 2000s, non-U.S. air force senior ranks were packed with officers for whom exchange tours with the USAF or USN had been a pivotal career experience. By 2024, multiple generations of leaders in early customer nations have that experience, and the first wave of exchange pilots from later customers has reached high rank. In some nations, retired senior officers with USAF exchange experience are high-level advisors to industry and government. The reluctance to break those links and associate with a new (and much smaller) air force with an unfamiliar culture is understandable.

One nation where familiarity with the U.S. was a major factor was, not surprisingly, Canada. After the traumatic cancellation of the Avro CF-105 Arrow in 1959, the Royal Canadian Air Force exclusively acquired U.S. combat aircraft, making the F-35 the logical candidate to replace the RCAF's F/A-18 Hornets, in the eyes of the

[101] https://wikileaks.org/plusd/cables/08OSLO670_a.html

Department of National Defence and the Conservative government of Stephen Harper.

However, Canadian law calls for all government procurement to be competitive: DND sought to bypass this process by declaring the F-35 to be the only acceptable solution. In the process, it developed a statement of requirements that was carefully crafted so that only the F-35 could meet them: for example, one requirement was for a 360-degree "zero light level" visual system, which ruled out night vision goggles and left an F-35-type EO-DAS as the only compliant solution. A scathing 2012 report by Canada's auditor-general put a stop to this plan[102].

Even then, in 2014, the Harper government approached the JPO with a proposal to "swap" F-35s in 2015 for future Canadian orders. This bold and questionably legal plan to pre-empt the decision process was leaked to the media[103] and promptly dropped. But the government's actions proved to be a poison pill for non-U.S. competitors, who subsequently put little effort into the Canadian competition.

Canadian Aircraft Options
Current Status

- **Canada swaps 4 LRIP 7 aircraft in CY15; payback with LRIP 9 aircraft**
- **Progress to date:**
  - AF concurred 4 aircraft swap is executable with 2 caveats:
    - USAF F-35 IOC remains on schedule – "No flex left"
    - If other partners make similar request, it would be difficult to accommodate
- **Next Steps:**
  - Canada needs to deliver Letter of Intent with updated beddown plan to F-35 PEO
    - ECD mid-November
  - Congressional Notification letter being staffed through JPO
    - ECD late-November

Another way to turn military experience into political support was found in Australia. The controversy over the 2008 South China Sea wargame received a good deal of public attention in Australia. Weeks later, the Williams Foundation think-tank was established, directed by a group of retired RAAF officers, but with Lockheed Martin as its principal sponsor: it is still a Platinum sponsor in 2024. The foundation immediately started to produce reports that reached pro-

102 "Stacking The Deck", Aviation Week, April 16, 2012
103 Guilty. (Author)

F-35 conclusions and promoted theories of warfare based on attributes of the F-35 system.

South Korea was another special case. In August 2013, the nation's Defense Acquisition Program Administration announced the selection of the Boeing F-15SE Silent Eagle – an F-15 with reduced radar cross section – for the nation's F-X3 fighter requirement. DAPA said that Lockheed Martin's F-35 bid had exceeded the program's cost limit.

An aggressive lobbying campaign followed, and within weeks the decision was reversed[104]. But, following the selection of the F-35, and with little publicity, Korean Aerospace Industries reached an agreement with Lockheed Martin under which the U.S. company would support development of the KF-21, a Korean-designed stealth fighter. Korea was the first nation to be offered such a deal.

Several F-35 buyers are participants in NATO nuclear sharing: Belgium, the Netherlands, Germany, Italy, and (before it was removed from the program) Turkey. The F-35 is the only current fighter aircraft, other than the Rafale, to be "dual role" equipped with nuclear weapon and control mechanisms. Since the U.S. has sole authority to develop and install the necessary equipment, these customers had no choice unless they withdrew from nuclear sharing – and in this matter, the Norway experience described above may be relevant.

F-35 marketing to foreign legislators includes briefings claiming that fighters other than the F-35 will be shot down in large numbers in a future engagement: For example: "If Canada buys 4th Gen Super Hornet or Gripen fighters and ever encounters the adversary that we face across the polar icecap or off the Western coast of British Columbia, Canadian fighters will get shot down, pilots will die"[105].

104 "Seoul Survivor", Aviation Week, September 30, 2013

105 https://billieflynn.com/f-35-war-gaming-fear-mongering/

In one interview in Australia, an LM pilot-marketeer said: """What we care about, as parents, is that we are going to send our sons and daughters into harm's way and what matters to us is that those men and women flying those fighter planes are coming home every single day."[106]

Whether or not this claim is accurate, it is unfalsifiable by many parts of the customer ecosystem, because it is asserted to be derived from highly classified wargames and the assessment of secret stealth technology.

This is a classic example of the marketing technique of fear, uncertainty and doubt (FUD), often associated with dominant companies such as IBM in the 1970s. It hinges not on the superiority of one's own product but on the catastrophic consequences of any other choice[107].

Another application of FUD concerns the reliability of support. Uniquely, the F-35 has a program of record in which production continues to 2052. Other aircraft, it is suggested, may become unsupportable, or costly to sustain, in the future.

Most defense contracts guarantee a fixed procurement cost but not sustainment cost[108], and as is well known, sustainment costs over a system's lifetime dwarf procurement costs. The seller will provide a projection of through-life costs but not normally guarantee it, so this is an area where the customer will assess the credibility of different claims. In the case of the F-35, the JPO and contractors have consistently predicted that the costs are on track to be reduced over time. A high estimate can be used to rule out a politically disadvantaged bid, as Norway did with the Saab Gripen E in 2008.

---

[106] https://www.9news.com.au/world/royal-australian-air-force-raaf-f35-fighter-jet-plane-williamton-newcastle/065f0d4f-67cb-40b3-a815-ab7ee359ca4e

[107] https://effectiviology.com/fud-fear-uncertainty-doubt/

[108] The exception is where the sale includes a high level of long-term contractor support, as in some Middle East deals.

Finally, the size of U.S. industry makes it possible to offer industrial benefits on a large scale – and JSF marketeers have not hesitated to inflate their market estimates while downselling their competition. A presentation to Canadian industry in 2013, for example, portrayed the end of all "4gen" production lines by 2022 and a sustained production rate of 225 aircraft per year[109].

Today, five other fighters remain in production, including Lockheed Martin's own F-16, and the JSF team – even when deliveries resume after the 2023 hiatus – is still struggling to produce 150 aircraft per year on schedule.

The full story of how the U.S. government supported and enabled F-35 sales may never be known, because much of it has taken place at diplomatic levels where confidentiality is integral to the culture. But to conclude from the lack of information that the pressures applied to Norway, Canada and Korea were outlier cases is not logical.

---

109 CF-35 For Canada, Keith P. Knotts, October 2, 2013

DESTINATION UNKNOWN

The status of the F-35 program was delineated in multiple Government Accountability Office (GAO) reports, Congressional hearings[110] and media summaries[111] in 2023 and 2024. There are several problem areas where the schedule, the cost, and – in some areas – the nature of a complete solution remains undefined, 22 years into full-scale development.

The current phase of F-35 development is known as Continuous Capability and Development Delivery (C2D2) and comprises two main activities.

- Technology Refresh 3 (TR-3) centers on a new Integrated Core Processor (ICP), memory unit and primary cockpit display, and is installed in all F-35s from Lot 15, which began to leave the production line in 2024.
- Block 4 comprises the update or replacement of avionics systems including the radar, electronic warfare system and the Distributed Aperture System. In 2023, there were 80 items in Block 4, with the last items delivered in Lot 23 in 2031, according to the GAO.[112]
- By 2023, Block 4 was expected to cost $16.5 billion in R&D.

In April 2024, it was disclosed that the Block 4 program was in disarray. Flight testing in an F-35 began in January 2023 but only 32 out of 205 planned sorties were accomplished in FY2023[113], and it was announced that tests were expected to continue past mid-2024. This has prevented deliveries of Lot 15 aircraft, which were placed in

[110] https://armedservices.house.gov/hearings/tal-hearing-f-35-acquisition-program-update

[111] https://aviationweek.com/defense-space/aircraft-propulsion/f-35-delivery-freeze-complicated-software-doubts-hardware

[112] "F-35 Joint Strike Fighter: More Actions Needed to Explain Cost Growth and Support Engine Modernization Decision", GAO May 30, 2023

[113] DOT&E report for FY2023

storage at an undisclosed location while the JPO worked with customers to explore whether an interim acceptable standard could be defined.

The first disclosure in April 2024 was that an interim "truncated" Block 4 package was due to complete testing in August/September, as long as testing did not result in the need for additional software drops. But this version of Block 4 is missing crucial capabilities and will not be combat-capable: this will not be fixed for another 12-16 months after the truncated package is released.

The problems with testing the first Block 4, it was revealed, have forced a complete redesign (called "reimagining") of the entire C2D2 program. No details were given, but the program will be slowed and downscaled to a subset of the original planned capabilities.

A subsequent GAO report issued in May[114] noted that "the scope of Block 4 will change as it becomes a major subprogram by removing capabilities that cannot be supported by the current F-35 engine and thermal management system": - that is many items would be deferred until the engine can be updated.

The report also criticized the JPO for not recognizing problems in time to order more test aircraft. The existing test fleet was aging, and unrepresentative of the current configuration – but new aircraft with full test instrumentation installed could not be delivered before 2029.

The extent to which Block 4 comprises new capability vs. fixes to Block 3 problems or diminishing manufacturing source issues is not known. GAO has asked for this information but has not received it.

The progress of C2D2 teaches some important lessons about the F-35 program:

- The centralized avionics architecture continues to result in delayed testing, with a high risk of unexpected problems.

[114] F-35 Joint Strike Fighter: Program Continues to Encounter Production Issues and Modernization Delays

With no partition between vehicle and mission management functions, tests of TR-3 were suspended until late 2023 because system crashes threatened flight safety, according to the GAO, "with some test pilots reporting that they had to reboot their entire radar and electronic warfare systems mid-flight to get them back online."

- This architecture has shown two characteristics, both on the F-22 and the F-35. Changes require extensive regression testing, to ensure that they have not affected other critical functions, Both ground laboratory testing and flying test bed work have proven to be poor predictors of how the system performs in the airplane itself.
- In December 2023, Lt. Gen. Michael Schmidt, the program executive office, said that he could not predict when a software issue that had halted aircraft deliveries since July would be corrected. "I wish I had all of the solutions in place that prove to me that when I do something in the lab, it's going to show up that way in the air," Schmidt told a Congressional panel.[115]
- Lockheed Martin's practice of "re-competing" subsystems, which was done with the ICP, adds risk if a competitor beats the incumbent on price, but does not understand the requirement, and injects an adversarial element into the relationship between prime, sub, and customer.

Further confirmation of problems with this architecture is that later programs have abandoned it. Instead, more processing is carried out in the subsystems themselves (which was not possible when the F-35 system was defined) and mission systems are separated or "partitioned" from flight-critical software. This technique is based on

[115] https://aviationweek.com/defense-space/aircraft-propulsion/f-35-delivery-freeze-complicated-software-doubts-hardware

commercial aircraft practice, was first implemented by Saab on the JAS 39E fighter, and has been adopted for the B-21 Raider bomber.

The cost and time to fix thermal issues is unknown. As noted above, Block 4 mandates upgrades that provide more cooling. The baseline plan adopted in late 2023 is to perform an Engine and Power Thermal Management System Modernization (EPM) program[116] to provide more cooling capacity while keeping temperatures within the engine. (The relationship between the PTMS and the engine is that the PTMS is driven by air bled from the engine and passing through a turbine. The more air bled out, the hotter the engine must run to produce the same thrust.)

For the engine, this is most likely to mean replacing the high-pressure compressor and turbine and the combustor - the hottest and most expensive parts of the engine. This part of the EPM program will be a sole-source contract to RTX. The same company's Collins Aerospace unit has announced its desire to compete with incumbent Honeywell for a new PTMS.

The cost of the EPM as a retrofit cannot be determined as yet. The F135 engine has a unit cost around $12 million. The core module, which incorporates the engine's hot components and exotic materials, will be at least half that. Honeywell has estimated the cost of a fleetwide PTMS retrofit program at $3 billion[117], and has warned that some approaches might require larger-diameter coolant lines, which would mean disassembling much of the structure and drilling larger holes in bulkheads and ribs. The full requirements for the engine and PTMS will not be available, the GAO reported in May, before the engine upgrade contract is awarded in late 2024.

EPM retrofits are almost certain to be mandatory. The need to bleed more air from the engine in the Block 3 configuration already

---

116 Program director statement to House Tactical Air-Land Subcommittee, Dec 12, 2023

117 https://www.aviationtoday.com/2023/08/15/replacing-f-35-ptms-may-cost-3-billion-honeywell-estimates/

shortens engine life, and there are associated operational limits, such on time spent in the low/fast envelope, and the need to retain enough fuel to act as a heat sink. Block 4 will exacerbate all these problems without the EPM.

Sustainment is posing major challenges. A GAO report published in September 2023[118] concluded that the JPO and the services had not implemented a coherent plan to contain sustainment costs, and that actions by the contractor team were keeping costs high. Notably:

- The contractors restrict technical data (which is their IP) to the extent that it prevents service personnel from carrying out sustainment tasks or training without direct contractor support.
- The process of tracking repaired parts is inefficient, so new parts are routinely used instead.
- One subcontractor withheld data from customer personnel, because it might be disclosed to Lockheed Martin and used to support a re-compete.[119]
- The DoD has planned to institute a performance-based logistics program for part supply and repair, but has not been able to show that it would save money or improve readiness.
- There are 14 different F-35 configurations in service.
- The Director of Operational Test & Evaluation reported in early 2024 that the mean flight time between critical failures for the F-35A in May 2023, after 289,000 flight hours, was half the threshold requirement set for 75,000 hours. Such failures took twice as many hours to correct as required. Both statistics were slightly worse than they had been in 2022[120].

[118] https://www.gao.gov/products/gao-23-105341

[119] This was very likely Honeywell on the PTMS.

[120] DOT&E, ibid.

- A further GAO report in April 2024[121] noted that mission-capable rates for the F-35, particularly for the Air Force fleet, are not only below threshold requirements but *have declined* since 2020; and that the services had met their sustainment cost targets, denominated in cost per aircraft per year, only by reducing their planned flying hours by 20%.

It is normal for a military aircraft to evolve during development, but almost unheard-of for model-to-model changes to result in R&D bills that are comparable to an all-new airplane. A 2030-model F-35 may from the outside be almost indistinguishable from a 2022-delivered aircraft, but the different avionics and other systems will mean that flight or ground crews can't be trained to fly both versions, and mission planning will be done differently. The software both onboard the aircraft, and on the ground (mission planning and maintenance) will be incompatible between the two versions.

That leads to complicated choices. It will be expensive, and possibly prohibitive in terms of personnel and capacity, to continue to support two or more different software and hardware standards indefinitely. That leaves two options.

- All pre-TR-3 F-35s can be upgraded. This was the initial vision, but the scope of TR-3/Block 4 has grown to the point where it poses problems. Even at a rate of 100/year, it would take ten years to upgrade earlier aircraft. That would require an upgrade line on the same scale as the new-production line, and would mean a near-doubling of supply of major subsystems – radars, engine cores, PTMS and more. There is no per-aircraft cost estimate for this, but older aircraft will need more upgrades.
- Some early aircraft can be replaced by new-production aircraft and be retired or transferred to second-line duties.

[121] F-35 Sustainment: Costs Continue to Rise While Planned Use and Availability Have Decreased - GAO-24-106703

This is already happening with pre-TR-2 aircraft, which are showing up in aggressor units. To some extent, this is not unusual in military aircraft production. But one problem is that partner nations such as Norway and Australia bought many of their aircraft in early blocks and will be disproportionately hard hit.

- A further issue affecting aircraft longevity may be on the horizon. In his April 2014 written statement to HASC, LTG Schmidt noted: "In February, F-35 stakeholders gathered for a Corrosion Summit, where team members identified new corrosion prevention initiatives to maximize mission capability across the fleet."[122] Australia had previously reported corrosion on F-35s associated with the use of 7085 series aluminum alloys, which are new to large-scale use in aerostructures, while U.S. Navy photos released in 2022 showed apparent corrosion on F-35s deployed aboard the USS Carl Vinson. (below).

122 https://armedservices.house.gov/sites/republicans.armedservices.house.gov/files/FINAL%20-%20Spring%202024%20HASC%20TALF%20F-35%20PEO%20Testimony.pdf

At this point it is legitimate to speculate as to whether a steady common configuration state can be maintained at all. For best interoperability and lowest sustainment costs, the desirable case would be to have one hardware configuration in production and being retrofitted, one legacy configuration in service, and a third in development, with the first two receiving regular software loads. Given the extent of hardware changes expected between 2022 and 2029 deliveries, and the continuing difficulty of developing and testing software (particularly the differences between lab and flight-test results) this goal may never be achieved.

Intellectual property issues will continue to affect both sustainment and upgrade efforts. With access to IP, customers would be able to bring more work in-house, and establish competition among contractors. But retaining IP is important to the contractors' financial health.

The F-35's drain on resources is affecting the ability to carry out future programs, on both the industry and government side. From 2006 to 2016, the U.S. aerospace industry was conducting one acknowledged major combat aircraft R&D program. It has been supporting two such programs since 2016, with the advent of the B-21.

New programs - NGAD, F/A-XX and CCA – were expected to bring the number to five, straining not only budgets but personnel – engineers who joined the industry in the booming Cold War years are reaching retirement age, at the same time as an expanding field of new-start aerospace programs offers new engineers a chance to work on fast-moving projects in small organizations without the oppressive climate of government security.

In mid-2024, it seems that both F/A-XX and NGAD will be delayed if not cancelled: at least in part, because F-35 now seems likely to require heavy R&D spending as well as procurement, through the early 2030s. As noted, Northrop Grumman had already withdrawn from a prime role in NGAD, leaving the Air Force choice between Boeing and Lockheed Martin.

This created an unusual competitive situation, due to the incentive structures left in the wake of the Last Supper. Because of its poor performance on earlier Air Force programs (the KC-46 tanker, T-7 trainer and Presidential Aircraft Replacement) and its weak financial condition, Boeing had no option but to submit a conservative, low-risk bid that the customer would believe.

Lockheed Martin knew this and would therefore not bid aggressively. But it would also have evaluated NGAD from the perspective of its likely impact on the F-35 program. Winning NGAD would not be good business for Lockheed Martin if the Air Force decided to cut back on high-margin procurement of the F-35 in favor of lower-margin R&D, with the risk of cancellation. But if Lockheed Martin competed and lost, it could throw its resources behind F-35 and lobby to delay or even cancel the new aircraft.

A third competitor would have changed the dynamic: Northrop Grumman had earned praise for its work on the B-21 and would have less concern about the impact of NGAD on F-35. But CEO Kathy Warden had pulled the company out of NGAD.

The result is that the USAF could have been faced with two high bids on NGAD, already reported to have a unit procurement cost close to $300 million, both hedged with terms favorable to the contractor team. In a turbulent political environment, such a program would very likely be cancelled.

Meanwhile, the Navy's F/A-XX project has been deferred, causing Northrop Grumman to shut down the division (named Apex) that it had dedicated to the project.

Combined with the chaos in the Block 4 program, this leaves the future of U.S. fighter development in disarray. Today, the only sure guess about the ending of the F-35 production line is that it will not happen as planned, in 2052.

LET'S NOT DO THIS AGAIN

Some of the experience described above should be translated into recommendations to improve future performance; otherwise, by default, lessons will have been taught by a Pavlovian process, based on what has been rewarded and what has been punished. As Berkshire Hathaway co-founder Charlie Munger put it so well: "Show me the incentives, and I'll show you the outcome."

Those default lessons will include:

- It is more profitable to defend an existing program than to compete in a new program.
- Underbidding on acquisition and profiting on sustainment is the preferred business model.
- Competition will take place at the first-tier supplier level and below.
- It is better to walk away than to question the requirement.
- Poor performance will seldom be punished and may be rewarded.
- Preservation of the industrial base is a prime directive; and no major company will be forced into an acquisition or allowed to fail
- Blatant dishonesty in public statements will not incur consequences, or even public pushback by the customer
- The threshold for termination is insurmountable.

It is clear that these issues are not confined to the F-35, which is simply the largest of defense programs and therefore has the greatest and widest influence. Other program issues affect only the U.S. Navy, Marines, or Army: the impact of the F-35 is global.

The question is whether this culture can be changed for any reason other than a geopolitical crisis with the U.S. on the losing side. However, it's possible to identify some paths for change.

The intent behind the following proposals is to improve the management of major, long-term programs by making the process more accountable and professional, and above all by establishing the correct institutional incentive structure. They are to some extent based on successful non-U.S. weapon-acquisition organizations such as Sweden's FMV and France's DGA, while recognizing that a national super-customer is a bridge too far for the U.S., and too ambitious to be realistic. The proposal can be outlined as follows:

- The DoD should begin to stand up permanent "acquisition executive organizations" (AEOs), each dedicated to the DoD-wide acquisition of major classes of systems, such as Air Combat Systems, Surface Warships, or Armored Vehicles.
- The AEO is accountable to DoD and is also tasked with informing and educating Congress.
- Service branches are the AEOs' customers, and each AEO is industry's customer.
- The AEO's **Prime Directive** is to deliver on time, on budget, and to spec, and to this end it works with industry and the services to set realistic KPPs, cost targets, and risk management strategies for each program.
- The DoD's role is to protect the AEO from budget fluctuations so that it can execute that mission.
- Once single-service programs have passed source selection, the AEO remains in the loop between service and industry, but with some delegation of responsibility to the service program office.
- The AEO's **Second Directive** is to maintain an acquisition strategy that contains suitable back-ups at every level. No single program should ever be without a reversionary plan until it provides a mature capability with stable and predictable costs.

- The AEO has extensive discretion over a reserve fund that can be used:
    - to reinforce, over the short term, program teams encountering unexpected problems
    - to launch quick-response innovative studies, as a VC accelerator or otherwise
- The AEO is tasked with maintaining the health of the supply chain and avoiding conflicts of interest between primes and suppliers.
- The AEO incorporates oversight of test and evaluation, and T&E accountability to Congress.
- The AEO hosts RCO-type organizations.
- The AEO is responsible for international strategy, exports and imports, and liaison with other government departments (State and Commerce), and is tasked with leveraging non-U.S. capabilities where these can support the DoD's mission.
- The AEO has authority and accountability to set security and clearance levels, and manage cybersecurity issues, with a directive to ensure security at the lowest practical cost.
- The AEO has a professional, career staff compensated at levels competitive with industry, augmented by rotating military officers and civilians. A path is provided for service officers with relevant skills to transition to the AEO.
- Within the AEO, each major program has an independent, part-time supervisory board of industry, service and technology experts, with its own staff.

Note that there are key differences between this and other current or proposed organizational constructs.

The AEO is accountable to DoD, not the customer. Its directive is not to pursue service desires but to match resources to goals and deliver on time; it is not under pressure to propose optimistic budgets and schedules in order to get programs approved. Staff and leadership are insulated, to the greatest possible extent, from the temptations of political office or private-sector employment.

It is the author's belief that reform on these lines, phased in one AEO at a time, would go a long way towards avoiding some of the issues that have afflicted the F-35 and other programs. It would foster a more rigorous pre-commitment scrubbing of requirements. It would provide distance and a firewall between service acquisition people and industry, with its phalanx of retired generals and its promise of post-service employment.

The AEO framework puts teeth into the DOT&E and budgetary watchdog roles, while unified and streamlined export, international collaboration and security rules could remove large overhead burdens.

Strategy at any level is about matching goals to resources, and there have been three overarching errors of strategy in the F-35 program.

The first is **a fixation on the progress of a program or a campaign vs. the strategy** - in his case, the completion of the F-35 program was prioritized over the maintenance of an effective TacAir force.

The second is that **no strategy can be successful, except by blind luck, without accurate information,** and the JSF program was plagued by optimistic forecasts and downplayed problems.

The third is that there was, at least for the U.S. Air Force, **no backup plan**.

Epilogue

It would have been better if this book never had to be written. Better decisions 30, 20 or even ten years ago would have resulted in a more effective conventional deterrent force today and a better prospect for 2030 and beyond.

Many people contributed to today's situation. Some had little power to influence matters, and some went along to get along. Some were entirely conscious of what they were doing and found it made them a good living. They know who they are.

But as Pyrrhus of Epirus said: "One more victory like that, and I would return to Epirus without a single soldier." We're out of chances to mess it up again.

APPENDIX: PERFORMANCE ASSESSMENT

Evaluating the capability of a military aircraft without access to classified information is not easy and is subject to analytical bias. But an experienced observer who has studied many different aircraft and come to conclusions that turned out to be accurate, given the best available data, can reach some broad conclusions that are not likely to be vastly inaccurate unless the system has important and completely covert capabilities. This sometimes happens (for example, no outside observer spotted the stealth features of the Lockheed Blackbird) but is rare.

Flight performance can be assessed based on weight, configuration, and engine characteristics. As noted earlier, STOVL design considerations and ship compatibility, combined with the need to carry internal weapons, limited the length of all F-35 versions and resulted in a low fineness ratio. The wingspan of the F-35A/B versions was also constrained.

The low fineness ratio was likely an important cause of the F-35's failure to meet transonic acceleration requirements, documented in the DOT&E's FY2012 report. Transonic acceleration from Mach 0.8 to Mach 1.2 for the F-35A version, was 8 seconds longer than predicted or required; 16 seconds longer for the F-35B; and 43 seconds longer with the larger-winged F-35C, an increase of about two-thirds.

Transonic acceleration is important because it is carried out at maximum thrust; drag peaks at transonic speed, reduces at slightly higher speed, and then increases gradually until it equals thrust, the theoretical max speed of the aircraft. Most fighters, however, are not tested to absolute max speed, because the time they can spend there before running short of fuel is ephemeral.

Instead, a tactically useful design and test limit is set: M=1.6 for the F-35. However, endurance at max Mach can be significantly reduced if too much fuel is used in transonic acceleration.

The F-35A/B configuration is an outlier among modern combat aircraft in featuring a small overall span (9 feet less than the Super Hornet, which has a similar empty weight to the F-35B) combined with a broad body. Much of the nominal 460 sq ft gross wing area is in fact body area; the net wing area is considerably less.

The aerodynamic effects can be easily seen in maneuvering flight in humid conditions. Droplet clouds form above the wing in a characteristic two-peaked shape, corresponding to pressure and lift distribution, and characteristic dense, tight vortices stream from the wingtips, both indicating high effective wing loading.

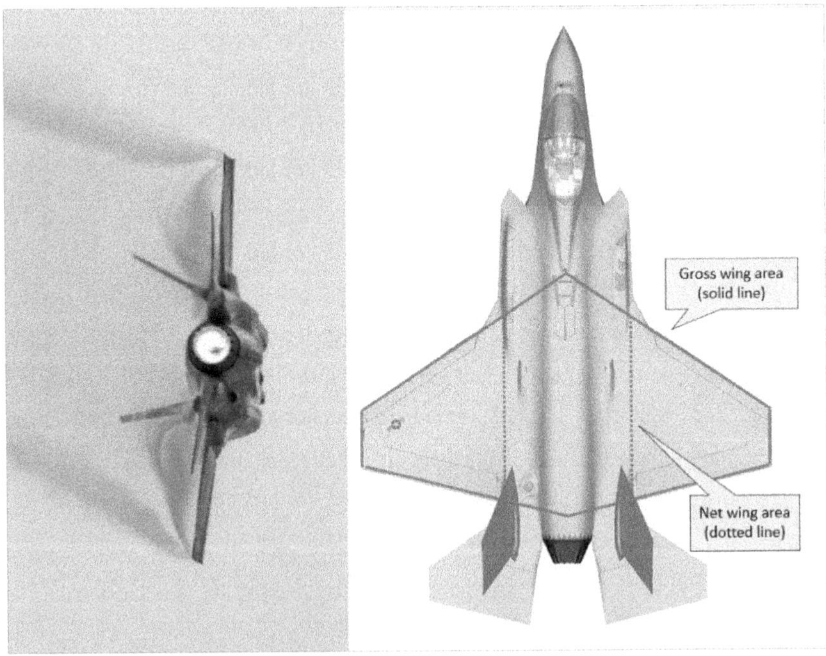

It was therefore predictable that a notorious 2015 test found that the F-35 by no means outclassed an older F-16 in basic air combat maneuvering. The type's air show performance is also what would be expected of a powerful, high-wing-loading aircraft: short maneuver sequences separated by accelerating level-flight runs along the show line to rebuild energy.

This is hardly surprising since the F-35 is designed around a large internal air-to-ground weapon load and stealth has been given priority from the outset.

However, high wing loading may also affect range with large payloads. A 2008 briefing to Norway claimed that "the F-35 has a radius of 673 nm on internal fuel alone and 728 nm using external tanks", only an 8 per cent difference for 32 per cent more fuel. (The tanks being considered at the time had a capacity of 425 US gal each, but development was discontinued.) This strongly suggests that adding weight and drag beyond the fully loaded clean condition has a disproportionate effect on efficiency – for example, take-off and climb might require more afterburner use, and initial cruise altitude might be lower, with heavier loads.

Internal loads and the reliance on stealth, it is argued, are the critical attributes of the F-35. So far, the most visible adversary measure to be taken against stealth – as applied to the F-35 – is the development of active electronically scanned array (AESA) radars operating in the VHF band. The fact that VHF radars are not defeated by the shaping techniques used on stealth aircraft such as the F-22 and F-35 is well known, but such radars were, in the past, unwieldy and slow-scanning. AESA overcomes this limit, and the Russian Nebo-xxx and Chinese JY-XX are also designed to hand-off targets accurately to UHF radar for more accurate tracking.

Such radars are not an ultimate answer. The radar-weapon combinations required to achieve a successful intercept are expensive (hence few in number) and large, making them easier to target or suppress: hence the development of a long-range anti-radar missile for the F-35.

However, a different radar threat to the F-35 has been identified. In a Collaborative Combat Aircraft (CCA) wargame conducted in July 2023 by the Mitchell Institute of Aerospace Studies, planners had to be aware that radars on Chinese KJ-500 airborne early warning aircraft and on surface action group warships form a radar defense-in-depth that will illuminate ingressing F-35s from the sides as well as in the front quadrant at lower frequencies than X-band, against which the aircraft is optimized. One result was that the unmanned CCAs had to perform defense-suppression measures against those threats.

The use of stealth in air-to-air (A2A) combat is another area where the technological goalposts have (not surprisingly) moved over the decade. The stealth fighter's goal is still to detect, identify, track and engage without warning, at least until the missile's active radar seeker lights up. As noted earlier, this is not simple and requires EMCON – minimal use of radar – and the fusion of active and passive sensors.

But the non-stealth adversary has changed. EMCON has been made more difficult as crude radar warning receivers have been replaced by wideband digital systems with much greater bearing accuracy and ability to detect a fleeting signal. Digital radio-frequency memory and phased-array transmitters have made jamming more effective, with more power in narrower beams. RCS-reduction measures mean still more power is needed to burn through the jamming and may eliminate some of the most reliable means of non-cooperative target recognition. Add a spritz of active cancellation through an AESA radar. And outside the RF band, the ability of high-performance infrared search and track systems to detect targets at range has been documented.

The author ticked off the above technology trends at a meeting in 2019 that was attended by Very Well Informed avionics engineers. The atmosphere turned somewhat chilly until a helpful colleague explained that your scribe did not have a clearance and was working from open sources.

There is no indication that the specified performance for the Block 3 configuration has been increased since it was defined in 2013. Clearly, the objective for Block 4 would be to compensate for changes in the threat since the program started, but the level of classification prevents any evaluation of its effectiveness. And, as reported, at the time of writing there is no firm schedule for the implementation of the 80-plus Block 4 capabilities, and some have been deferred until after the engine and cooling system upgrades have been delivered.

F-35 TIMELINE

January 1986	US-UK Advanced STOVL study agreement signed at NASA Ames Research Center, California
Fall 1986	DARPA awards classified ASTOVL study to Lockheed Skunk Works
January 1988	DARPA issues follow-on contracts to Skunk Works, General Dynamics and McDonnell Douglas for conceptual stealthy STOVL Strike Fighter (SSF) designs
1989	Initial US-UK ASTOVL concepts evaluated and fail to meet operational needs
1990	DARPA awards study contracts to Pratt & Whitney and General Electric for STOVL lift systems including (respectively) shaft- and gas-driven lift fan systems.
1992	DARPA issues RFI for ASTOVL ground demonstrator programs based on lift fans
March 1993	DARPA issues Common Affordable Lightweight Fighter (CALF) demo contracts to Lockheed and McDonnell Douglas, including large-scale powered ground-test models. The plan is to flight-test one design in STOVL and CTOL versions. .
July 1993	"Last Supper" meeting heralds defense consolidation Boeing releases details of AVX-70 STOVL fighter; in March 1994, commits to match USG funds for a demo program to DARPA requirement
September 1993	Clinton administration cancels future combat aircraft studies (Navy A/F-X and USAF MRF) and forms of Joint Advanced Strike Technology (JAST) program
December 1993	UK and US officials announce that UK will join the CALF program.
August 1994	UK-US CALF MoU signed. Lockheed and Martin agree to merge, deal closed in March 1995

October 1994	CALF is merged into JAST under MG George Muellner, as basis for single future fighter, in three vanants, for USAF, USN, USMC, UK-RN and other export customers.
Mid-1995	JAST defines demonstration program. • Two competing aircraft to be flown, with downselect in 1996. • Northrop Grumman, McDonnell Douglas, British Aerospace form JAST team based on lift-plus-lift/cruise concept • Boeing and Lockheed compete separately
March 1996	RFP issued for JAST Concept Demonstration phase, response deadline in June. Program name changed soon after to Joint Strike Fighter.
November 1996	JSF awards to Lockheed Martin (X-35) and Boeing (X-32). Each to build two demonstrators to represent STOVL, CTOL and CV configurations, while designing Preferred Weapon System Concept (PWSC) aircraft for engineering and manufacturing development (EMD) program.
December 1996	Northrop Grumman and British Aerospace join Lockheed Martin team Boeing announces planned acquisition of McDonnell Douglas
February 1997	Contracts awarded to P&W and GE/Allison/Rolls-Royce for JSF engine EMD. P&W F135 to power Concept Demonstration aircraft and early JSF deliveries; GE F136 to compete from later Lots.
January 1999	Italy joins JSF program as observer
2000	Final downselect slipped to 2001
September 28, 2000	Boeing X-32A makes first flight
October 24, 2000	Lockheed Martin X-35A first flight
July 2, 2001	Boeing X-32B completes STOVL envelope, but with part of inlet and landing gear doors removed

July 20, 2001	Lockheed Martin X-35B performs "Mission X" – STO, supersonic acceleration, VL
October 26, 2001	Lockheed Martin awarded EMD contract • F-35 designation assigned due to mishearing • First flights of all versions in 2006 • IOCs: USMC FY10, USAF FY11, USN/UK FY12 • 300 production aircraft by 2012 • FRP funded 2012: 110/year USAF, 84/year USN/USMC
June 2002	Australia joins JSF program
2003-2005	PDR discloses unacceptable weight increase leading to redesign. • Original design AA-1 to fly end 2006 • F-35B first flight mid-2008, F-35C 2009 • IOCs slipped by two years • DoN procurement cut, 1089 to 680 • Full rate cut: 80/year USAF, 50/year DoN • Final USAF delivery slips to FY2038
2006	Production, sustainment and follow-on development (PFSD) MoU signed by UK, Australia, Canada, the Netherlands. Denmark, Italy, Norway, Turkey follow by 2009.
September 2006	FY2007 budget • USAF funds LRIP-1 for two F-35As • Administration proposes to cancel GE/RR F136 engine, blocked by Congress until 2011
December 15, 2006	F-35 AA-1 first flight
June 2007	F-35C Critical Design Review complete • Empty weight growth to 34,800 lbs. • Wing area increased to 680 sq ft
June 11, 2008	F-35 B-1 first flight
November 2008	Norway confirms choice of F-35

April 2009	Defense Secretary Bob Gates caps F-22 production at 187 aircraft; later, in speeches in Chicago and Fort Worth, expresses high confidence in F-35 program.
February 1, 2010	Gates fires JPO director MG David Heinz and launches three-year review of program. Schedule and IOC dates tentative pending review. Flight test sorties restored to program
June 6, 2010	F-35 C-1 first flight
August 2010	Israel approves purchase of F-35
October 2010	UK Strategic Defence and Security Review announces that CATOBAR will replace F-35B.
December 2011	GE and RR end efforts to save F136 Quick Look Review reveals multiple open problems Japan orders F-35
May 2012	UK reverts to F-35B, citing ship modification costs
June 2013	JPO commits to new IOC dates: F-35B December 2015 in Block 2 configuration • F-35A December 2016 in Block 3.1 configuration • F-35C February 2019
November 2013	South Korea reverses selection of F-15 and announces choice of F-35
July 2015	USMC declares IOC with F-35B
November 2015	Air Combat Command vice-commander says that USAF will limit growth in annual orders pending arrival of Block 4 configuration, may order more F-15s
August 2016	USAF declares IOC with F-35A
September 2017	2018 budget (heralded by 2018 SAR) reduces projected sustained rate: USAF 60/year, DoN 45/year. Final USAF delivery in FY2044
February 2019	USN declares IOC with F-35C

March 2019	USAF FY20 budget caps annual procurement at 48 aircraft through FYDP, final delivery in FY2052
January 2020	Poland orders F-35
December 2021	Finland orders F-35
September 2022	Switzerland orders F-35
December 2022	Germany orders F-35
April 2024	Block 4 update program scaled back drastically due to overruns and delays

www.ingramcontent.com/pod-product-compliance
Ingram Content Group UK Ltd.
Pitfield, Milton Keynes, MK11 3LW, UK
UKHW021923190726
13853UKWH00002B/819

9 798324 580780